DRY STONE WALLS

History and Heritage

Angus J. L. Winchester

AMBERLEY

To Val, with much love

First published 2016

Amberley Publishing
The Hill, Stroud
Gloucestershire, GL5 4EP

www.amberleybooks.com

British Library Cataloguing in Publication Data.
A catalogue record for this book is available from the British Library.

ISBN 978 1 4456 5148 4 (print)
ISBN 978 1 4456 5149 1 (ebook)

Typesetting and Origination by Amberley Publishing.
Printed in Great Britain.

Contents

Detail of the nineteenth-century wall at Gatesgarthside, Buttermere, Cumbria.

Acknowledgements

Across the years numerous colleagues and former students have helped me develop my thinking about the history of dry stone walls by pointing me towards sources and passing on relevant information. In particular, I should like to thank Tony Breakall and Mary Rose, Anita Carrieri, Derek Denman, David Johnson, Tom Lord, Jamie Lund, Bill Shannon, Nigel Smith and Ian Whyte. The author and publishers also thank the following people and institutions for supplying and granting permission to reproduce images for which they hold the copyright: Chris Bratt of the Dry Stone Walling Association (Cumbria Branch), Yorkshire Archaeological & Historical Society, North Yorkshire County Record Office, Historic Environment Scotland, Eric Jones, and Colin Smith.

Abbreviations

CAS   Cumbria Archive Service
CWAAS   Cumberland & Westmorland Antiquarian & Archaeological Society
TNA   The National Archives, Kew
YAS   Yorkshire Archaeological Society

Introduction

Dry stone walls create much of the character of upland landscapes across Britain. To the Yorkshireman J. B. Priestley, they were part of the essence of northern England. 'When I see them, I know that I am home again', he wrote in *English Journey* (1934), going on to say that 'no landscape looks quite right to me without them.' He was thinking of the soot-blackened gritstone walls behind Pennine mill towns, but the same is true of dry stone walls of different character elsewhere. The pale grey limestone walls of

Dry stone wall country at Muker, Swaledale, North Yorkshire: an archetypical landscape of dry stone walls and field barns in the Yorkshire Dales.

the Yorkshire Dales, gleaming white in the sunshine, and the darker slate walls of the Lake District are integral parts of those much-loved landscapes, as well. And it is not only true across northern England: the stane dykes of Scotland; the boulder walls of Northern Ireland; the limestone walls of the Cotswolds, the Mendip hills and the Isle of Purbeck in southern England; all these contribute to the distinctive character of those areas. Wherever stone is in abundance, it has been used to create boundaries between fields and alongside lanes, whether in the British Isles, in the dry rocky lands around the Mediterranean or in the high kingdoms of the Himalayas. In the British landscape dry stone walls are synonymous with the uplands, replacing hedges as the predominant form of field boundary as soils thin and stone becomes more abundant. 'They run', wrote Priestley, 'from the edges of the towns to the highest and wildest places on the moors, firmly binding the landscape.'[1]

Yet dry stone walls puzzled Priestley, as they puzzle many others: 'Who built these walls, why they were ever thought worth building, these are mysteries to me', he wrote. This book is an attempt to offer some answers. When were dry stone walls built, why, and by whom? How do we go about dating them? The following pages explore these questions and also suggest how walls themselves may be 'read' as historical evidence, shedding light on past farming practices and the history of local communities. The first part of the book traces the history of dry stone walls from medieval times to the present. The standard form of most walls probably dates from Tudor times but the great era of wall-building in the uplands took place comparatively recently, in the eighteenth and nineteenth centuries. The second part of the book looks at dry stone walls as

A dry stone wall under construction. Note the sloping batter of the wall in cross-section (shown by the frame), the two rows of facing stones with 'throughs' to tie them together and packing stones (or 'hearting') to lock them. (© Chris Bratt, Dry Stone Walling Association, Cumbria Branch)

part of Britain's cultural heritage. The walls themselves contain evidence of why they were built and how they functioned as part of the farming system. They sometimes preserve information about their builders and owners or evidence of lost features in the landscape. Although this discussion takes in the history of walls across the length of Britain, the focus is unashamedly on northern England, which possesses some of the highest concentrations of dry stone walls.

When looking at dry stone walls from an historical perspective, it is helpful to use modern walls as a benchmark. Since the eighteenth century, most dry stone walls constructed across Britain have followed a more or less standard pattern. Standing approximately 4 feet, 6 inches (1.4 m) high, the wall is a 'double wall', consisting of two faces, with their constituent stones pinned together by smaller locking stones that form a core of rubble. Stability is provided by rows of 'throughs', stones placed across the width of the wall, tying the two faces together. Larger stones at the base form a foundation layer and the wall tapers from approximately 30 inches (750 mm) at the base to 15 inches (400 mm) at the top. The wall is completed by a row of capstones, often set vertically. These construction features are found regardless of the type of stone used, so that walls that appear very different at first sight may be structurally almost identical. As this book shows, 'standard' dry stone walls tend to be comparatively recent, replacing other styles of walling constructed in earlier times and reducing the richness of regional diversity in the use of stone that was formerly found in field boundaries across the uplands of the British Isles.

1

The History of Dry Stone Walls

A. Walls in the Landscape

How old are dry stone walls? This is often the first question that springs to mind but it is one to which there is no short answer. Taking a long view, it is clear that most walls are part of a comparatively modern farming landscape, which cuts across the earthworks and other relict features of older landscapes. In parts of the Yorkshire Dales the tumbled field boundaries of late prehistoric or Romano-British field systems underlie the modern

Field walls cutting across the lynchets of a Romano-British field system at Malham Cove, North Yorkshire.

walled fields, which bear little relation to them. The walls are part of the historic, rather than the prehistoric, landscape. Indeed, it is sometimes clear that they are the latest incarnation of the farming landscape, overlying not just prehistoric fields but medieval features as well. In the Nent valley, near Alston in the North Pennines, for example, a multi-period relict landscape, containing both Iron Age or Romano-British settlements and fields systems, and medieval ridge and furrow, is overlain by the stone-walled enclosures of the modern fields; this suggests that the walls are of post-medieval date and represent a rewriting of the landscape. Elsewhere, however, dry stone walls can be shown to be part of a landscape of field boundaries that have evolved over many centuries and have their roots in the middle ages, if not before. In such areas, historians and archaeologists have taken a variety of morphological approaches to untangling the age of dry stone walls. Absolute dating is often difficult, though several authors have suggested that particular styles of walling or distinctive features in their construction can be dated to particular periods, as discussed below.

A useful starting point when charting the history of dry stone walls is to distinguish between the two complementary categories of land found in most upland farming systems: the cultivated land and hay meadows on the valley floor, on the one hand, and the hillside pastures, on the other. These two land-use zones each possessed a distinct history, histories that are reflected in the age and character of the dry stone walls found in each. The boundary between the two, known as the 'head-dyke' or 'ring-garth', took the form of a substantial and permanent barrier, which was arguably one of the earliest elements in the farming landscape of the uplands. The first land to be separated

Post-medieval field walls overlying the complex earthworks of a Romano-British settlement and the medieval ridge and furrow at Banks, near Alston, in the North Pennines.

Head-dyke (or 'ring garth') at Newlands, near Keswick, Cumbria. Note the vegetation contrast in either side of the wall that divides the old farmland in the valley floor from the common grazings on the open hillside.

and protected by physical enclosures would be the precious plough land and meadow, which produced the food on which man and beast depended; a first priority would have been to construct a head-dyke to keep livestock out of the growing crops. Land within the head-dyke will have been worked since the medieval period, if not before, with the modern field pattern being the product of evolution over many centuries. By contrast, the hill grazings outside the head-dyke remained unimproved and undivided, and, in many places, were used communally until comparatively recently. Parts of the hills were separated from the common as shared pasture enclosures in the sixteenth and seventeenth centuries but much remained as unenclosed common land until the great wave of enclosure under acts of Parliament in the later eighteenth and nineteenth centuries; some, indeed, remain unenclosed today.

Both on the map and on the ground, the contrast between walls in the 'ancient enclosures' within the head-dyke and those resulting from Parliamentary enclosure is striking. The professionally surveyed, straight, uniform walls of Parliamentary enclosure abut against the curving, sometimes meandering walls of the earlier fields. Building materials differ: Parliamentary enclosure walls are generally built of quarried stones; earlier walls contain rounded, irregular stones gathered in the process of field clearance. Since the 'ancient enclosures' were the product of evolution over the centuries (in contrast to the single-phase construction of the Parliamentary enclosure landscape), they tend to be characterised by variety in the form taken by field boundaries: dry stone walls are often only part of a landscape that includes hedges, field banks and fences.

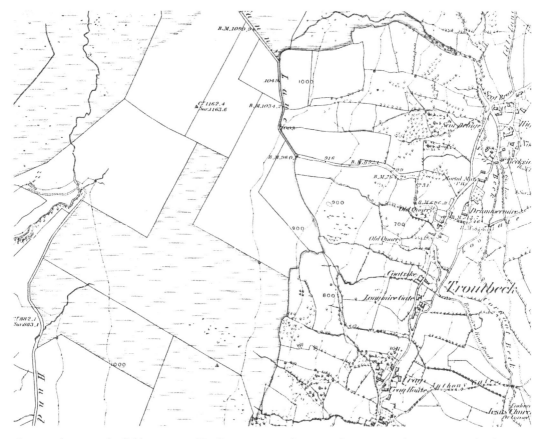

Contrast between the field patterns of Parliamentary enclosure and 'ancient enclosures', Troutbeck, Cumbria. The difference between the rectilinear fields on former common land, enclosed in 1842, and the older fields closer to the village is striking. (Ordnance Survey Six-Inch map, Westmorland sheet XXVI, surveyed 1859).

Thus the field pattern of farmland within the 'ancient enclosures' forms a multi-period landscape. The head-dyke or ring garth often stands out as a primary boundary, with the internal field boundaries representing secondary subdivisions of the plough land and meadows. Outside the head-dyke there were often 'intakes', land taken in from the edge of the common, forming obvious accretions abutting the primary boundary. A detailed analysis of field boundaries at Hebden in Wharfedale, undertaken by the Hebden History Group, provides a good example. The group identified four large primary enclosures around the village, probably representing former head-dykes enclosing cores of farmland. The large enclosure to the south-west of the village, in particular, appears to delineate one of the village's medieval open fields, the fields within it taking the form of narrow strips that are typical of piecemeal enclosure of open fields. Outside the primary enclosures, a scatter of dwellings set in irregular fields on the moorland fringe probably represents intaking around squatter settlements. Then, finally, the land stretching across the moors away from the village and its fields was divided into rectangular walled enclosures in the 1850s.

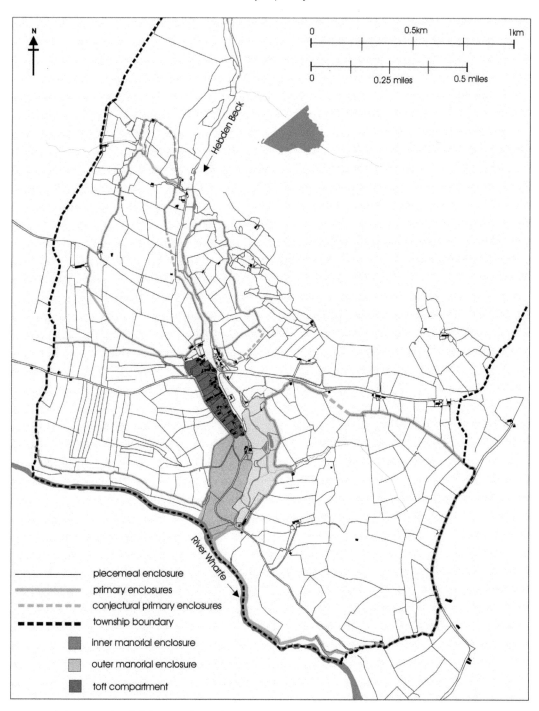

Hebden in Wharfedale, North Yorkshire: primary enclosures identified from a survey of field boundaries carried out by the Hebden History Group. (Reproduced by permission of Yorkshire Archaeological & Historical Society; map courtesy of Trevor Croucher)

Hebden illustrates the main components in the history of dry stone walls in upland areas of northern England: the establishment of primary boundaries (head-dykes) to separate cores of farmland from surrounding pastures, the subdivision of arable land and meadow within the head-dyke, extensions of the enclosed area by taking in parts of the lower slopes of the hills, and finally the wholesale enclosure of moorland commons. The rest of the first part of this book examines these processes in greater detail.

B. Medieval Walls

Many walls in areas of 'ancient enclosure' look old: their irregularity, and their moss-covered and lichen-encrusted appearance give them a look of having grown organically out of the landscape, having been there for many centuries. But how many walls in the modern landscape can be identified as truly medieval features? Indeed, to what extent were dry stone walls a feature of the medieval landscape of upland Britain? When reconstructing the medieval landscape at the micro-level, it is important to remember that there would have been far fewer field boundaries than in the modern landscape. Not only did moorland and fell lie open and unenclosed but much of the farmland within the head-dyke would have consisted of communally organised arable land and meadows, in which the shares of individual farmers lay open to one another. The annual rhythm of farming meant that the year was divided into a 'closed' season, where fields were made secure to protect the growing crops from livestock, and an 'open' season, where field boundaries were thrown open in the autumn to allow all the community's livestock to graze across the farmland within the head-dyke. Even in areas with little open-field land, where enclosed fields were the norm, the tradition of an 'open season' seems to have survived until the sixteenth century.

The process of identifying medieval walls and establishing how much of the modern landscape of dry stone walls is inherited from the medieval centuries is fraught with difficulties. On the one hand, old walls will have been repaired frequently (and sometimes rebuilt wholesale) across the centuries, as sections have shifted and collapsed, so that little of the initial walling may survive unchanged, though a wall's foundation layer is less likely to have been replaced. On the other hand, a wall may well represent the rebuilding of an earlier field boundary of a different type. This means that documentary or map evidence showing that a particular field had been enclosed by a certain date does not necessarily provide evidence for dating the wall surrounding it, as the wall may have replaced an older barrier several centuries after the field was initially enclosed. Some of the lines followed by walls may thus be of considerable antiquity, even if the fabric of the boundaries themselves is comparatively modern.

A relative chronology can sometimes be established by carrying out a 'T-junction' analysis to identify primary boundaries that are respected by other, arguably later, boundaries. This form of analysis, carried out both on the map and in the field, underlay the work of the Hebden History Group in Wharfedale. When such an analysis of the field pattern is accompanied by an analysis of field-names, it is sometimes possible to reconstruct the sequence of enclosure. For example, Thwaites, in the upper reaches of the Calder valley in west Cumbria, consists of an island of enclosures on the edge of unenclosed fells, a medieval clearing that contained four farms in the sixteenth century.

How old is a wall? Only the concrete paving slabs used as throughs and a slight change in colour show that this section of wall in Wensleydale, North Yorkshire, has been rebuilt in recent times.

'T-junction' between two walls near Longsleddale, Cumbria. The newer wall (coming in from the left) clearly abuts against an existing wall (running away from the camera).

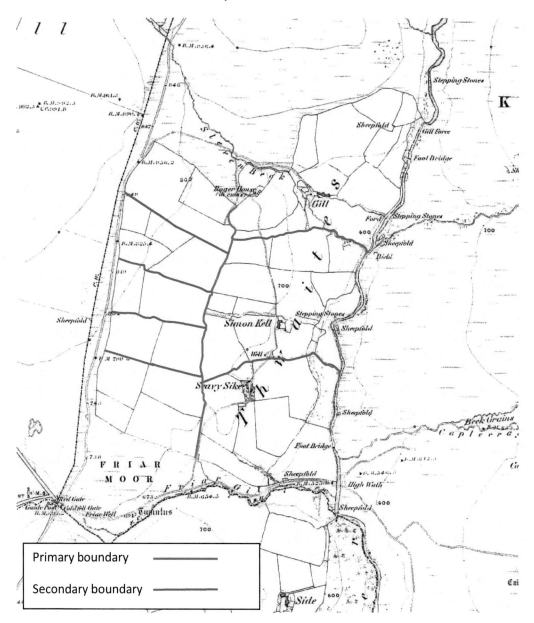

'T-junction' analysis of field boundaries at Thwaites, Kinniside, Cumbria. The primary boundary divided the older core of fields (on the right) from land newly enclosed from the moor in the mid-sixteenth century (on the left). (Ordnance Survey Six-Inch map, Cumberland sheet LXXIII, surveyed 1860–1)

A 'T-junction' analysis of the field pattern suggests that a boundary running north–south through the enclosures is a primary boundary, while a number of secondary boundaries (themselves respected by other boundaries) run out from it. Documentary evidence shows that the primary boundary marked the western limit of enclosure before an additional block of fields was taken in from the common moorland at some date between 1547 and 1578, almost doubling the size of the farms. In the nineteenth century, the names of the fields perpetuated the memory of the contrasting histories of the areas either side of the primary enclosure: while the older enclosures to the east bore a range of names, almost all those in the area taken in in the mid-sixteenth century contained the element 'moor' (Rough Moor, Low Moor, Far Moor, etc.). Most of the secondary boundaries coincided with the boundaries between the farms, reflecting the pattern of landownership. In this instance, it is possible to marry documentary and morphological evidence to reconstruct something of the history of enclosure, but this is not often the case.

Documentary evidence rarely sheds much light on the nature of medieval field boundaries. Numerous estate records (surveys, estate accounts, for example) survive from the thirteenth century onwards; however, before *c.* 1550, they present the landscape in financial, rather than topographical, terms, recording the value of rents and services yielded by particular parcels of land, rather than giving details of their physical character. Where they are mentioned, field boundaries are often described using the Latin term *fossatum,* meaning something dug – its root is *fossa,* 'a ditch or trench', probably translating to the vernacular 'dyke', which was used both in the

Manorial boundary across open fells between Rydal and Grasmere, Cumbria. By 1581 it had been marked by an earthen bank (visible in the foreground) and stone wall (in distance; now collapsed).

sense of a ditch and of an embankment. The description of a boundary at the head of Ribblesdale in the heart of the Yorkshire Pennines in 1543 as a *murus sive fossatum* ('wall or dyke') suggests that 'dyke' was being used to refer to a field wall, as remains the case in Scotland. Minor place names sometimes record the presence of stone walls in the medieval landscape; not far away, on the hill pastures of Newby, near Clapham, the name 'le Standik' ('the stone dyke') was recorded in around 1170 and confirms the existence of at least some stone boundaries at that early date.[2]

In a few instances it is possible to marry documentary evidence and field archaeology. A manorial boundary across the Lake District fells between Grasmere and Rydal, which had been defined in 1277, was described in 1581 as taking the form of a dry stone wall in parts and an 'earthen dyke' further uphill; both can still be seen in the landscape today. Likewise, documents record the division of hill pastures at Brown Willy on Bodmin Moor, Cornwall, between hamlet communities in the later medieval period, creating large blocks that are now marked by substantial stony banks more than 1 metre high or by earth banks with wide ditches.

One type of settlement that might be expected to yield evidence for the nature of medieval field boundaries are the seigniorial demesne stock farms, for which documentary is sometimes particularly full. Two upland 'vaccaries' (lordly cattle ranches)

Gatesgarthside, Buttermere, Cumbria. The nineteenth-century wall was successor to the massive, heather-covered earthen bank on the left, which was probably the boundary of the medieval 'park of Gatesgarth'.

illustrate the challenges of marrying documents to the landscape. At Gatesgarth, at the head of the Buttermere valley in the Lake District, a vaccary had been established by the 1280s, exploiting the flat valley floor to grow hay for winter feed and the broad fellsides as summer grazing for the cattle.[3] The large bank of fellside known as Gatesgarthside can be identified as the 'park' of Gatesgarth, which formed part of the vaccary there in the 1280s. However, the boundary of the 'park' seems to have had several incarnations since then. The present wall probably dates from the 1850s; an earlier wall was said to be ruinous by the early nineteenth century. It, in turn, had probably replaced a massive earthen bank, perhaps the medieval boundary, which survives in part.

In the Pennines, another vaccary, that belonging to Marrick Priory on moorland at Owlands in Swaledale, was said in 1585 to have been 'all enclosed with a stonne wall'; however, other contemporary documents make it clear that, by that date (almost half a century after the Dissolution of the priory), there were within the former vaccary 'divers dykes stoone walls and enclosed medowe grownds now at this daye decayede and not mainteinedde'. There was also 'an olde dyke or casten stoones of an olde wall'.[4] The impression is that the medieval vaccary contained a mixture of boundary types, which

Marrick Priory's vaccary at Owlands, in Swaledale, North Yorkshire, which is recorded as having been enclosed with stone walls by 1585. The wall dividing meadow ground (to the right) from moorland probably replaced an earlier bank (visible beside it), though whether the modern wall is one of those recorded in 1585 is unknown.

were by that date falling into decay. The dry stone walls of the modern landscape presumably represent a later rebuilding; certainly, the modern stone wall separating the meadows at Owlands from the moorland seems to have replaced an earlier earthen bank, traces of which survive beside it. At both vaccaries, it seems likely that some, at least, of the medieval enclosures took the form of banks rather than walls.

Taking a morphological approach – identifying differences in the shapes and building style of walls, with a view to establishing a typology of dry stone walls – presents further challenges, not least the problems posed by rebuilding, noted above. It must also be borne in mind that different raw materials may have lent themselves to varying construction techniques, so that what appears to be a distinctive style dating from a particular period may rather be a distinctive response to particular geology. Bearing these difficulties in mind, it has to be said that few attempts to identify distinctive features of medieval walls are wholly convincing.

In several studies, two characteristics have been identified as typifying early walls: the use of large boulders in the foundations and the inclusion of large stones placed vertically, known as orthostats (literally stones 'standing on their backs'), which contrast with the horizontal coursing of modern walls. Stony banks containing rows of orthostats have been found in association with known medieval sites in the uplands. Medieval field systems at Brown Willy on Bodmin Moor, Cornwall, were divided by low stone banks, not dissimilar to the field boundaries associated with a late-medieval farmstead at Rannerdale in the Lake District, which take the form of low walls, little more than a single course high, containing orthostats. In these cases there is little to indicate that stone

Footings of relict wall containing orthostats associated with deserted medieval farmstead at Rannerdale, Cumbria.

has been robbed – these boundaries may never have approached the height of a modern dry stone wall. The stones surviving from such medieval walls may have been only part of the original structure, as it is likely that the low stone courses would have been topped by some form of additional barrier, probably a 'dry hedge' of stakes interwoven with brushwood, which was a common form of field boundary before the seventeenth century. However, the difficulties of linking a particular construction feature to a specific period are reinforced by the linking of orthostats to different chronological eras. At Roystone Grange, in Derbyshire, double rows of orthostats with a rubble fill were identified as being Romano-British, while at Bransdale in the North York Moors orthostats show some correlation with the field-name 'intake', suggesting a post-medieval date.

In the case of a second feature – the presence of large boulders in the base of a wall – the grounds for suggesting an early date rely on the assumption that larger stones would be rolled to the edges during field clearance and incorporated into the base of walls when fields were first enclosed. It could thus be argued that such walls are likely to be of a comparatively early date, though absolute dating is rarely possible. At Hebden in Wharfedale, the oldest walls surrounding the four primary enclosures (probably of medieval date) were characterised by the presence of large boulders, some set as orthostats. More generally, large boulders are often found in walls surrounding what are arguably early cores of arable land, reinforcing the conclusion that their presence in field walls may be taken as an indication of age.

Boundary of one of the primary enclosures at Hebden in Wharfedale, probably medieval in origin. Note the boulders in the base, some of which are orthostatic, and the distinctive projecting coping stones.

Boulders forming the base of wall near Peel promontory, Crummock Water, Cumbria. The wall encloses the site of a medieval manor house and may be medieval in origin.

Detailed morphological analyses of walls themselves have also attempted to identify distinctive walling styles of medieval date. A pioneering investigation of a dry stone wall landscape at Roystone Grange, Derbyshire, by Martin Wildgoose and Richard Hodges, identified a distinctive form of wall as being medieval in date. These were low walls, approximately 3 feet (1 m) high, the fabric consisting mainly of single rows of large boulders of dolomitic limestone. Few sections survive in what was postulated to be their original form, most having been incorporated into later walls. The authors claimed that the presence of the large dolomitic boulders (readily identified from the limestone fabric of later walls by their brown colour and rounded shape) was the key diagnostic feature of medieval walls in the area, and mapped the distribution of walls containing them. The pattern of walls containing these boulders was striking: they were found in the primary boundaries that formed the outer perimeter of the Cistercian grange but were otherwise restricted to a group of smaller enclosures around the buildings at the heart of the estate.

In the limestone country of Craven, Tom Lord and David Johnson have recently identified a different style of wall in the Malham and Ingleborough areas as being earlier than standard dry stone walls and as being possibly of medieval date. These are wide-topped walls with near vertical faces, sometimes topped with distinctive flat projecting top stones; some incorporate massive orthostats. More substantial than

Wall at Roystone Grange, Derbyshire, identified as medieval in origin. From a typological analysis of walls in the area, Martin Wildgoose and Richard Hodges suggested that this was one of the walls dating from the twelfth or thirteenth century. The diagnostic feature is the presence of large boulders of dolomitic limestone (standing out as darker and rounder than the quarried limestone).

standard walls of post-medieval date, they were built up to 6 feet (1.8 m) high, were 30 inches (70–80 cm) at base and around 20 inches (50 cm) wide at the top. An early date is suggested by the fact that many form primary enclosures (and stand out as distinctly different from the standard construction of the secondary walls abutting them), and some appear to relate to grazing grounds belonging to monastic houses in the medieval period. However, absolute dating is far from clear. In all these examples, the extent to which walls that exhibit suggested early features are inherited directly from the medieval period is unclear, not least because so many will have been rebuilt across the centuries.

Clearer evidence for walls of medieval date comes from land retained for lordly use, in particular from deer parks, which were walled from an early date. A stone wall (*murus lapideus*) was built anew around the Bishop of Durham's great park at Auckland Castle in 1350, and a park wall (*murus parci*) is recorded at Thringarth Park in Teesdale from the fifteenth century, when it needed repair. By the sixteenth century, new lordly enclosures were regularly separated by a wall. In the Lake District, the 'New Frith' at Wasdalehead – a woody bank of fellside enclosed in the mid-sixteenth century for the lord's deer – was 'walled about', while Holme Wood at Loweswater had been enclosed

Wide-topped wall with near vertical sides and flat capstones projecting on each side, at Over Pasture, Selside, near Horton-in-Ribblesdale, North Yorkshire. This is the distinctive style of wall in the Craven limestone identified as medieval by Tom Lord.

Massive wall forming the eastern boundary of Thringarth Park, near Middleton-in-Teesdale, Co. Durham, probably part of the 'park wall' (*murus parci*) recorded in estate accounts from 1440.

Park wall at Ravenstonedale, Cumbria. A late example of a lordly park wall, this massive structure was built for Thomas Lord Wharton between autumn 1560 and November 1561.

'with ditch and wall' in the later sixteenth century. Impressively high walls surrounded Lord Wharton's new deer parks at Wharton, near Kirkby Stephen, and Ravenstonedale, both built in the mid-sixteenth century. Even in the uplands, however, not all parks were walled: Troutbeck Park, near Windermere, was said in 1607 to be partly 'walled with a litell wall' and partly 'hedged & fenced with a litle stike hedge' (probably a 'dry hedge' of the type described above).[5]

Several tentative conclusions may be drawn. First, in a landscape in which so much land was used communally for at least part of the year, permanent field boundaries were comparatively few in the medieval period. Second, with the exception of deer parks and some other lordly enclosures, dry stone walls of the modern type were probably rare before the sixteenth century. Diagnostic features of early walls may include the presence of large boulders and orthostats, though absolute dating is often impossible. Locally distinctive types of walling may have existed, such as the low boulder walls proposed at Roystone Grange or the wide-topped limestone walls of parts of Craven, although, again, clear evidence of dating is scarce.

C. Walls in Old Farmland

By the sixteenth century we begin to encounter more frequent documentary references to walls as field boundaries. In part, this reflects the increasing attention to the physical character of landed property that emerged in documents at this time, but there is also evidence that walls were becoming more common. The period between *c.* 1500 and *c.* 1750 saw a major change in the landscape of field boundaries, involving the renewal of existing boundaries and the creation of permanent, stock-proof enclosures, whether 'quick' (i.e. living) hedges or walls. This was the physical expression of a revolution in the farming system, which involved a move towards private property and away from communal organisation of farmland. The cumulative result of enclosure in upland areas across the early modern period was no less than a 'great rebuilding' of field boundaries in old farmland.

This rebuilding often took the form of dry stone walls. From the first half of the sixteenth century, orders appear in the records of manorial courts from Craven (Yorkshire) and the Eden Valley (Cumbria), requiring tenants to build or replace existing boundaries, particularly the head-dykes surrounding arable land, with stone walls. In 1526 , at Helton in the Eden valley, each tenant was to make five roods of the 'ryng garthe' with a stone wall sufficient to keep out cattle; at Yanwath, near Penrith, each tenant was ordered in 1532 to rebuild annually two roods of the dyke around the field in stone 5 feet (152 cm) high; four years later, the tenants at Calton, near Malham in Craven, were each required to reconstruct one rood of the boundary between the fields and the moor with a stone wall. These are early examples of orders that continued

Former head-dyke at Yanwath, near Penrith, Cumbria. In 1532 the manor court ordered the dyke around the field to be rebuilt in stone. The large boulders at the base of the wall are probably an indication of antiquity, even if the upper part of the wall has been rebuilt since.

to be made into the early seventeenth century. Two aspects stand out: first, the courts appear to have been initiating a rolling programme of wall-building, particularly along the head-dyke or ring garth. This was made explicit in an order from Shap, Cumbria, in 1592, wherein the tenants of Rayside and Tailbert, on the edge of the fells in Swindale, were required to 'make all their outlying dikes of their feild sufficiently in stone wall foure foot high, & to make sixe roods of the same every years until such time as the same be made round about.'[6] There thus appears to have been a conscious effort to replace older boundaries with substantial permanent dry stone walls. The second striking feature of these manor court orders is that where they specify the height of the wall to be built, it is comparable to modern walls, often 5 feet (152 cm) or 'six quarters' (4 feet, 6 inches; 137 cm), suggesting that walls similar in dimensions to modern walls were not uncommon by 1600.

One distinct form of walled enclosure, combining a wall and a bank, was also used for head-dykes in parts of northern England in the sixteenth century. This was a dyke 'breasted' with stone, a substantial earthen bank faced with a wall on one side to keep livestock out. Some manor court orders specified that this type of boundary was to be built. In 1573, for example, the court of Lune Forest in Teesdale ordered each tenant to

Stone-breasted bank forming the head-dyke between the farmland of Haile and common land on Cold Fell, near Egremont, Cumbria.

make up part of the dyke surrounding the lord's close '& brest yt with stone'. Similar orders are found from villages along the Pennine edge of the Eden Valley: a dyke in the fields at Renwick was be 'breasted with stone' in 1587, and in 1602 Ousby court ordered each tenant to make one rood of the head-dyke with 'breestede stone wall'.[7] In the Lake District, two boundaries, which can be dated to the middle decades of the sixteenth century, take exactly this form. At Thwaites, discussed above (pp. 16–17), the block of land taken in from the moor in the mid-sixteenth century is enclosed in part with such a boundary, the stone 'breast' facing the common. The bank, around 1 metre high, is now surmounted by a post and wire fence, and would have required some superstructure, probably originally a 'dry hedge', to make it stock-proof. A very similar boundary survives, though now tumbled and decayed, around a bank of hillside, deep in the fells at Buttermere, called Bleak Rigg, which was enclosed by a group of farmers *c.* 1568.

Stone-breasted bank at Friar Moor, near Egremont. The fields on the right were taken in from the common in the mid-sixteenth century, which probably gives an approximate date to this boundary bank.

One driver in the move to renew and heighten boundaries may have been agrarian change, particularly changes in livestock management, which required boundaries to be permanently sheep-proof. A low wall topped by a dry hedge would be sufficient to control cattle and horses, whereas a more substantial structure would be needed to be stock-proof against sheep. A particularly interesting comment, given in evidence during a lawsuit concerning the boundary across the Lake District fells between Ambleside and Rydal in 1581, draws the distinction between walls capable of turning cattle and those able to keep sheep in. The boundary had been marked by a wall of some description by the early sixteenth century: an octogenarian witness told how 'duringe all the tyme of his remembraunce' the wall running up the boundary to Low Pike had been maintained to prevent movement of horses and cattle ('for weareinge out of great goods as horse and cattall') until sixteen years previously (that is *c.* 1565), when it was agreed that it should be made secure against all animals: 'for holdinge oute of all manner of beastes wanderinge and goinge to the one ground frome the other'.[8] Until then, sheep had been managed by herds and the implication is that less intensive herding had made it necessary to modify the wall. The wall, built *c.* 1565, is probably that which survives today (unless, of course, it has been comprehensively rebuilt since the sixteenth century).

Boundary wall between Rydal and Ambleside, Cumbria, rebuilt to make it sheep-proof *c.* 1565. Note the wide top and the overhanging 'cams' (capstones) on the near side of the wall to deter sheep from Ambleside straying onto Rydal's fell.

It is a striking wall, substantially larger than most standard dry stone walls. Standing 5 feet, 6 inches (around 1.7 m) high to the underside of the capstones for much of its length, it is approximately 24 inches (60 cm) wide at the top, with capstones overhanging on the Ambleside side. It is therefore comparable in size to the wide-topped walls of the Craven limestone sheep pastures.

A similar distinction between cattle-proof and sheep-proof walls is hinted at in another lawsuit, this time concerning the boundary between Barton and Martindale, beside Ullswater. There, a wall erected in the early sixteenth century was said to have been made 'for stopping of great cattall', implying that it was not intended to be sheep-proof.[9] Although these are only isolated comments, there may well have been a functional distinction between walls to protect against the movement of cattle and horses, on the one hand, and those capable of turning sheep, on the other. The low walls identified from the medieval period were presumably intended to control cattle and horses, whereas modern dry stone walls, which seem to have their roots in the sixteenth century, were intended to prevent movement of sheep.

Another factor may have been legal. Much of upland northern England was notionally designated as hunting forest during the medieval centuries and some of the seigniorial privileges associated with forests and chases continued to be upheld. One of these was that no enclosures should be made that prevented deer from having free movement across the whole of the forest, including the farmland of settlements within it. There is some evidence that this notion was still recognised in the sixteenth and seventeenth centuries. Marwood Hagg, a hunting ground near Barnard Castle, Co. Durham, was divided in two in the late 1630s by building a wall, which, though claimed to be five quarters (3 feet, 9 inches; 115 cm) high, was in fact 5 feet (152 cm) tall in places, which was deemed too high, as it hindered the movement of deer.[10] It may well have been that walled field boundaries in medieval hunting forests were required to be low, like the low walls topped with dry hedges, of which field evidence survives. If so, the increasing frequency of dry stone walls of the modern type from the sixteenth century may also reflect the final abandonment of legal restrictions in former hunting forests and chases.

The process of open-field enclosure went largely unrecorded in the uplands but appears to have gathered pace from the late sixteenth century to the eighteenth. Arable land and hay meadows, which had been held as open, unenclosed strips by neighbours, were gradually divided, sometimes by consolidating ownership through a process of exchange, each farmer then enclosing his share. The result was often a pattern of long, narrow, strip-like fields, preserving the shape of the open-field furlongs. The distinctive reversed-S 'aratral curve' of open-field ridge and furrow was ossified in the new boundaries, as the precise line of each landowner's new enclosure was dictated by the pre-existing pattern of property rights. Such landscapes of piecemeal enclosure in former open fields are found widely across northern and western England. In lowland areas such as the Solway and Lancashire plains, the new enclosures took the form of banks and hedges, but, on the upland margins and into the hills, stone walls become more common. Particularly striking are the landscapes of limestone walls surrounding villages in the White Peak of Derbyshire, where strips of narrow fields running out from the village tofts preserve the layout of the open fields. A comparable process lay behind open-field enclosure elsewhere. The very different field pattern at Wasdale Head in the Lake District seems to have been the product of enclosure of an open field shared by eighteen farms in the late sixteenth century, which had disappeared by the eighteenth.

Wardlaw, Derbyshire, in 1982: a landscape of narrow, strip-like enclosures preserving the distinctive aratral curves of strips in the former open fields. (P. L. Winchester)

Litton, Derbyshire. The sheer volume of stone consumed in walling the narrow crofts behind the village street is remarkable.

Enclosure of former open fields at Tideswell, Derbyshire. The open fields here had been largely enclosed before 1730.

Wasdale Head, Cumbria. Documentary evidence suggests that the pattern of small, irregular, stone-walled fields is the result of the enclosure of an open field, probably in the seventeenth century, though the field pattern itself and the presence of large clearance cairns hint at a more complex process.

The cumulative effect of open-field enclosure and piecemeal renewal of field boundaries was a reconstruction of the farming landscape within the head-dyke to produce the walled or hedged patchwork of fields, which often survives today. Much of it took the form of small-scale activity on landed estates and yeoman farms across the seventeenth and eighteenth centuries, as farmers repaired and rebuilt walls, renewing boundaries along alignments determined by pre-existing patterns of ownership and land use.

Estate records chart something of this process. In the Charterhouse area of the Mendip Hills in Somerset, the estate accounts of the Gore family record the making of new walls between fields and the repair of existing walls in the 1670s. At the other end of the country, the Westmorland gentleman Sir John Lowther (d. 1675) of Lowther committed considerable time and money to walling around his demesnes in the mid-seventeenth century. What prompted his expenditure is hinted at when he described the activities of his father, Sir John (d. 1637), who 'new walled' the demesnes near Whale, including the boundary of Rowlandfield, which was 'all formerly stick and dry hedge, and was in continuall repairinge, and spent much wood.' The capital cost of a solid stone wall would be offset by the savings incurred through no longer having the constant repair of a 'dry' hedge. From the 1640s to the 1660s, the younger Sir John replaced the 'smale low wale' around Rowlandfield (presumably built in his father's day) with a massive wall, 11 quarters (8 feet, 3 inches; 2.5 m) high, which involved employing thirty to forty men all winter, gathering stones and walling. Similarly, the 'ill Coble wale' round another parcel of the demesnes, which was ineffective at keeping the sheep off the common, was replaced by a new wall in 1669. Some of the stone required for the new walls came from a programme of field clearance, thus improving the quality of the land while securing its boundaries at the same time: in 1652/3 Lowther 'gott all the earthfast stones I could out of the Millfeild, which it was full of ... I bestowed the best of the stones in waleinge about it.' But quarried stone was also needed: when he replaced one 'old coble rewenus wall' with a new wall in 1656, he got the stone from 'a very goodly quarie' where stone had been 'never sought for before'. The references to 'cobble' walls suggests that earlier field boundaries, which had utilised field stones, were being replaced by larger, more solid walls using better stone.[11]

A similar story of piecemeal renewal appears in the records of yeoman farms in Cumbria. Clement Taylor of Finsthwaite in Furness Fells undertook several bouts of walling on his estate in the 1720s and again in 1743, employing wallers on a piece-work rate (at between 7d and 10d per rood), anticipating the piece-work system that became the norm during the period of Parliamentary enclosure in the nineteenth century. One of the new walls was specified as being 5 quarters (3 feet, 9 inches; 115 cm) high below the 'cams' (i.e., capstones), comparable in height to modern Lake District walls.[12] The west Cumberland yeoman diarist, Isaac Fletcher of Underwood, Mosser, recorded a programme of investment in field boundaries over a quarter of a century, probably replicating a process that went on unrecorded on yeoman farms across the region. In the mid-1770s he employed wallers on some of his higher land; however, locating a supply of suitable stone was a major headache. In 1776, a quarry on his own land close to the intended new wall proved to be inadequate but he obtained 'fine stones, which put up the wall pretty fast' from a neighbour's quarry. Walling another field two years later, he was forced to use stones that were 'very bad and very slow to work'; they were so thin and small that he predicted 'it will be very tedious as well as expensive.'[13]

Walling was a task of the winter and early spring, occupying the dead time in the farming calendar to ensure that walls were in good repair in readiness for the closing of fields and meadows to keep livestock from the growing crops. Taylor's walling took place between November and February; Fletcher's largely in March. On the Fleming estates at Rydal in the 1690s, spring saw groups of wallers employed to repair the 'outwalls', presumably the boundaries with neighbouring landowners. Typically, a fortnight's work each year at 4*d* per day (plus tobacco) for each workman was enough to keep the walls in good repair.[14]

In summary, the use of dry stone walls as field boundaries in old farmland increased dramatically between 1500 and 1750 as a result of the interplay of several processes. The spread of walls may be viewed as part of a general rebuilding of field boundaries in those centuries, both in a shift from the impermanence of dry hedges to more durable boundaries and in the enclosure of open fields and meadows. But that in itself does not explain the emergence of the 'standard' dry stone wall at this time. If the modern dry stone wall is essentially intended to be a sheep-proof boundary, its emergence may be associated with the development of sheep husbandry. The key may lie in a move away from intensive herding of sheep, whereby the absence of staff-wielding teenagers tending the flocks required boundaries, which would keep sheep where they were wanted.

D. Intakes and Cow Pastures

The sixteenth and seventeenth centuries also saw an increase in the amount of enclosed pasture in northern England, allowing for greater sophistication in the management of hill grazings. From the later medieval period through to the eighteenth century, large acreages of pasture were enclosed from the lower hillsides. There was considerable regional variation in this process: in the Pennines, many communities enclosed communal cow pastures by throwing a wall around a bank of hillside to separate it from the higher moorland. Elsewhere, in the Lake District for example, the process mostly involved small-scale 'intaking', where individuals took possession of sections of the lower fells behind their farmsteads.

In the Yorkshire Dales many hundreds of acres were enclosed from the lower slopes of the Pennine moors as communal stinted cow pastures that belonged to groups of local farmers. In Wensleydale and Swaledale, each hamlet possessed a stinted pasture covering a section of moorland beyond the fields, and there, as elsewhere, the outer boundary of the pasture took the form of a dry stone wall. The process of enclosing these pastures was attenuated. Some appear to have been separated from the open moors by 1600 – cow pastures in Swaledale were said to have been enclosed in the early sixteenth century – but elsewhere there is clear evidence of continuing enclosure in the seventeenth century. In 1612, for example, the tenants of New Houses in Bishopdale had set out a 363-acre (147-ha) section of hillside to be enclosed as a cow pasture, while the tenants of Hanging Lund and Hellgill, high in the fells at the head of Mallerstang, were enclosing part of their common as late as 1694. These were communal efforts and usually entailed building a wall to separate the shared cow pasture from the open fell, as is shown graphically on a late-seventeenth-century map of Askrigg in Wensleydale, where 'Askrigg Old Pasture' and the 'New Inclosure' are both shown as walled

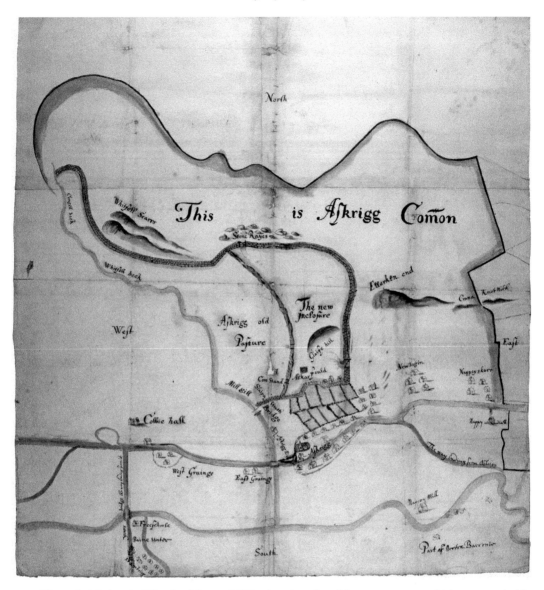

Plan of Askrigg in Wensleydale, *c.* 1675, showing the old cow pasture, which was probably enclosed in the sixteenth century, and the 'new inclosure' added to it in the early seventeenth century. The stone walls separating them from the common contrast with the hedged fields closer to the village. (Reproduced by permission of The North Yorkshire County Record Office. Reference ZOA 45)

enclosures. Being communal enclosures, all those with an interest in the cow pasture shared responsibility for building and maintaining the outer wall, sections being allotted to individual graziers. A tangible legacy of this sometimes survives in the presence of wall heads and marker stones that indicated the point where one man's responsibility ended and his neighbour's began (see pp. 79–80).

In most cases such communal cow pastures were later subdivided between those who had a share: where this happened, the walls of the inner divisions are of a later date than the outer enclosure. A trade developed in the stints (or 'cattlegates') that gave a right to graze a certain number of animals on the pasture, resulting in the concentration of grazing rights in fewer hands. By the later eighteenth century the numbers of interested parties had often declined, making it easier for private agreements to be made dividing the pasture between individuals. Such division of stinted pastures by common consent often left no documentary record but agreements such as those from Troutbeck (Cumbria) in 1744 and Settle (North Yorkshire) in 1757 show that the process was under way by the mid-eighteenth century.

In the Lake District communal cow pastures were less frequent, though not unknown. Near Buttermere, for example, a 311-acre (126-ha) bank of fellside called Scales can be traced back as an enclosed pasture to the fifteenth century. In the early seventeenth century, thirteen men held grazing rights in it for milk cows in the summer months and for young sheep ('hoggs') over winter. What form the enclosing boundary took at that time is unclear: the latest incarnation of the wall separating it from the common was

Twisleton Pasture, near Ingleton, North Yorkshire. The rocky hillside was probably separated from the common in the sixteenth or seventeenth centuries; its outer enclosing wall runs along the skyline. In 1755 the valley side remained an open shared pasture but, by the mid-nineteenth century, it had been divided into sections by a series of roughly parallel walls running upslope.

probably built in the 1740s, when the manor court ordered one to be built. In most Lakeland valleys, enclosures on the lower fellsides usually took the form of intakes – piecemeal extensions of the enclosed acreage, created by individuals. The process had begun by Tudor times: at Grasmere the tenants had taken in parts of the common across the 1570s, enclosing their intakes with 'walles hedges and ditches'. A similar process can be charted elsewhere: in many valleys, additional rents paid for small fields, known in the language of estate surveyors as 'improvements', can be traced back to the mid-sixteenth century.

The process continued in some places into the eighteenth century. In Eskdale the manor court had assigned to each farm an area on the lower fells, close to the farmstead, as a pasture for its milk cows, when it laid out regulations to govern grazing rights in 1587. This had the effect of giving individual farms exclusive grazing rights over an adjacent piece of fellside and, by 1700, several farms had enclosed the areas assigned to them in the sixteenth century. The resulting intakes are invariably enclosed by walls built of stone from the rock-strewn slopes. In the late eighteenth century this process led to disputes. The inhabitants of Boot and a neighbouring farmer, Thomas Tyson of Borrowdale Place,

Buttermere Scales, a stinted pasture in the Lake District. Recorded from the fifteenth century, it was shared by thirteen tenants in 1614, who grazed cows there in the summer months and young sheep across the winter. The present wall probably dates from around 1740, when the manor court ordered a new enclosing wall to be built.

Intakes on the lower fells at Eskdale, Cumbria. The field perched under the crag on the right had been enclosed by 1578, when it was described as an 'improvement' called 'Kidman Garth', for which a separate rent was paid.

Intakes on the slopes of Yewbarrow at Wasdale Head, Cumbria. Some of these 'improvements' had been enclosed before 1664.

Slighted wall of an intake at Boot Bank, Eskdale, Cumbria, enclosed in the 1780s. This was an intake too far: after a lawsuit it had to be thrown open to the common again.

made two large intakes on Boot Bank in the 1780s; however, they were forced to throw them open to the common again as a result of opposition from other farmers, as they not only reduced the area of the common but also blocked the route that the manor court had assigned to a neighbouring farmer for driving his sheep to the fell. The tumbled remains of these intake walls survive, slighted at regular intervals to allow sheep to ignore the boundary. Evidence given in the lawsuit by the waller who built Tyson's intake describes a remarkable degree of informality in the enclosure process. Crispin Pharaoh told the court that he had started the wall in about 1782 and it took him four years to complete the full length of 1,200 yards (1,100 m). There were, he said, 'no marks whatever ... to go by'; he simply built it 'where it was most convenient to get stone'.[15]

E. The 'Age of Improvement': Parliamentary Enclosure Walls

The majority of dry stone walls in Britain date from the 'age of improvement', the century from *c*. 1750 to *c*. 1860, which saw a major rewriting of the rural landscape in many parts of the country. In upland areas of England and Wales, this transformation involved the enclosure of thousands of acres of common pasture on the hills and moors through the process of Parliamentary enclosure, whereby statutory powers were granted to commissioners to enable commons to be converted into private property. Common rights were abolished, and those who had a legal interest in the land subject to enclosure were allocated sections of the former common in lieu of their rights. Blocks of land were assigned to the lord of the manor as owner of the rights in the soil and to the local commoners who had exploited the common by exercising their grazing rights and other rights, such as the right to cut peat or to gather bracken, rushes and heather. Many thousands of metres of dry stone walls, from the Cotswolds and Mendip hills in the south, to the length of the Pennine chain from Derbyshire, to Cumbria in the north, were built across former common land as part of this process. Throughout England and Wales, 6.8 million acres (2.75 million hectares) were subject to Parliamentary enclosure, but this figure includes wide swathes of open fields in Midland counties. In the six northern counties of England (excluding the East Riding of Yorkshire), where most enclosures during this period involved rough grazing land on the hills, almost 1.5 million acres (over 600,000 hectares) of commons and wastes were enclosed, representing a substantial proportion of the land surface: 26.5 per cent of Cumberland; 20.8 per cent of Westmorland; almost 16 per cent of Northumberland; and 13 per cent of the West Riding. In upland areas, the landscape of old farmland, discussed above, was largely left untouched by Parliamentary enclosure, so that the walls of the new enclosures on the moors and fells abutted on an older pattern of field boundaries on the lower slopes.

The new landscapes created by these processes were laid out on drawing boards in the offices of land surveyors. The new fields were generally large rectilinear enclosures with

Parliamentary enclosure of moorland at Oxenhope, near Keighley, West Yorkshire. The wide strips of straight-sided fields, enclosed in 1774, contrast with the unenclosed heather moorland of Haworth Moor behind.

straight boundaries – a marked contrast to the smaller irregular fields of earlier centuries. An enclosure award was drawn up by the commissioners tasked with converting the former common into private shares and laying out occupation roads to provide access to the new fields (termed 'allotments'). An accompanying plan laid out the boundaries of the allotments in detail, showing responsibility for building and maintaining the boundary fences and placing a time limit on completing the initial enclosures. Across upland Britain the division of hills and moors was realised by teams of professional wallers building mile upon mile of new dry stone wall. The resulting pattern of walls often seems to lie uncomfortably across the land surface, being a rational layout of field boundaries laid out across the broken ground of the fells and moors.

In Scotland, a different legal basis to landholding enabled landowners to refashion their estates without recourse to enclosure acts. The spirit of improvement (a drive to maximise the productivity of the land by reclamation, land drainage and scientific farming) encouraged lairds to dispossess their tenants and to lay the land out afresh into larger consolidated holdings, a process that had begun in south-west Scotland by the 1720s. The Highland clearances were only one aspect of a much more extensive

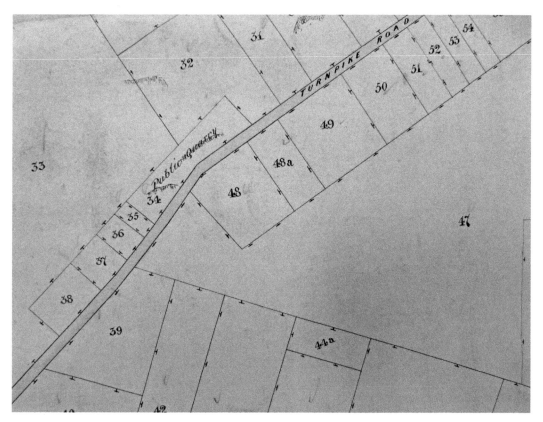

Parliamentary enclosure allotments on Ash Fell, near Kirkby Stephen, Cumbria, laid out on the enclosure award for Kirkby Stephen Common in 1855. The 'T' symbols indicate responsibility for building and maintaining the new walls. Cumbria Archive Service (Kendal), WQR/1/50. Reproduced by permission.

Landscape of Parliamentary enclosure at Troutbeck, Cumbria. The rectilinear fields and the wide, walled occupation road were laid out when the common, known as The Hundreds, was enclosed in 1842.

rewriting of the Scottish landscape, which gathered pace across the eighteenth century. The new landscapes of improvement were laid over both old farmland and hill grazings, resulting in a more fundamental reorganisation of the land than occurred in upland England. Substantial new walls cut across and replaced the older rubble walls of the farming townships, substituting the intimate irregularity of the 'fermtoun' for a landscape of right angles and straight lines. The process continued well into the middle decades of the nineteenth century in the Highlands. At Clashmore in north-west Sutherland, for example, the rectangular 'parks' of a model farm laid out in the 1870s represent a late example of such remodelling.

Where enclosure and reclamation went hand-in-hand, the back-breaking task of stone-picking from the newly ploughed land would yield stone for the new walls – indeed, there was an over-abundance in some places, where stone needed to be consumed by broad 'consumption dykes' (see pp. 56–7). But where, as was often the case in upland areas, the new walls divided tracts of unimproved rough grazing, adequate supplies of stone could come at a premium. Many enclosure awards reserved a suitable piece of the common as a public stone quarry; some explicitly gave landowners the right to go into any part of the former common to take stones for the initial burst of wall-building. In

Improvement-era walls cutting across the pre-Improvement landscape at Brockloch, Glenesslin, Dumfriesshire. The deserted farmstead and its surrounding fields enclosed by banks and tumbled walls are overlain by large rectangular enclosures with an associated suite of sheepfolds. (© Crown Copyright: Historic Environment Scotland)

at least one case, that of Lorton (Cumbria), where the commons were enclosed in the 1830s, conflict over stone supplies arose when the lord of the manor's agent prevented allotment holders from digging stone on their own allotments, on the grounds that the enclosure award reserved all mineral rights to the lord.[16]

Gathering stone formed a major part of the cost of walling. In the late eighteenth century, a waller might expect to be paid around 2 shillings per rood of 7 yards (6.4 m) – roughly a day's work for building a wall. However, the full cost, including carting stone, would be at least 6 shillings. In the Mendip hills of Somerset, the price of

Clashmore, Stoer, Sutherland. The large rectangular fields bounded by Galloway dykes were laid out when a model farm was established in the 1870s.

dry stone walling per 'rope' of 20 feet (6.1 m) in the 1790s was put at 8*s* 3*d*, made up of 2 shillings for quarrying the stone (eight loads at 25 cwt each); 4 shillings for hauling it to where the wall was to be built; and 2 shillings for building the wall, with an extra 3 pence for covering it with a turf topping (a local alternative to capstones). Even with the cost of quarrying and hauling stone, a dry stone wall was considered to be cheaper than a hedge and, of course, it provided an instant stock-proof boundary.[17]

By the late eighteenth century the standard modern dry stone wall was becoming the norm across England, a process no doubt accelerated by the increasing numbers of professional wallers employed to build the new walls. In Wensleydale in the 1750s, we hear of John Dinsdale of Snaizeholme, who had a small farm but whose chief source of income was 'building and repairing wall fences, the grounds and lands in this part of the country being inclosed and fenced with walls and not with hedges'.[18] The young diarist Charles Fothergill, visiting Wensleydale in 1805, recorded walls built by professional wallers that were almost identical to modern walls. It is striking that he noted 'great improvements have of late been made and more skill and knowledge of mechanics [are] observable' and his description of 'a modern stone wall in these dales' implies that it would have differed from older walls. In form the 'modern' walls he saw were about 6 feet (1.8 m) high (including the capstones), tapering from 24–30 inches (60–75 cm)

Wensleydale, North Yorkshire, already a landscape of dry stone walls by the 1750s.

at the base to around 15 inches (38 cm) below the capstones, with two or three rows of throughs; then, as now, walling frames and guide lines were used to maintain the profile.[19] Identical dimensions are recorded in the Mendips in the 1790s.

Precise specifications, sometimes spelt out as requirements in enclosure awards, confirm these dimensions. Two or three layers of throughs were specified. Height was typically to be between 4 feet, 6 inches and 6 feet (1.37–1.8 m); width was around 30 inches (75 cm) at the base and 14–16 inches (35–40 cm) at the top. By 1800, therefore, the evidence points towards an increasing uniformity in walling styles, as preferred practice (or fashion) spread, fostered by the specifications laid down in enclosure awards, the interchange of agricultural ideas among landowners, and the accumulated skill and knowledge of an increasing army of professional wallers. In England the norm became the standard design of dry stone wall still built today. In Scotland a comparable process saw the distinctive Galloway dyke spread out from its homeland in the south-western counties to other areas (see pp. 54–5).

By the mid-nineteenth century the dry stone wall landscape was largely complete. Indeed, the very latest enclosure awards, dividing some of the highest and craggiest land in the Lake District in the 1860s and 1870s, were put into effect not by building walls but by adopting the new technology of sturdy wire fences on iron strainer posts. The remains of these survive, for example, on the fell-top watershed between the Ennerdale

Wardlaw, Derbyshire, in 2016. Noticeably fewer dry stone walls survive, particularly to the right of the clump of trees in the centre of the image, than in the view taken in 1982 (p. 31).

and Buttermere valleys, marking the outer boundary of Ennerdale Fell, which was enclosed in 1872.

Since then the modernisation of farming has tended to lead to the decay of dry stone walls. As the land increasingly came to be held in fewer, larger farms, while mechanisation and a steep decline in the farm labour force reduced the number of hands available to maintain walls, many dry stone walls became redundant in the modern farming system. Some walls have been actively removed to create larger fields but, more often, they have been left to deteriorate as stock graze across several fields that are now thrown open and treated as one. A survey of dry stone walls for the Countryside Commission in 1996 reported that perhaps half were no longer stock-proof and were derelict or heading towards dereliction, while only 13 per cent could be considered fully sound and stock-proof. Something of the effect of this loss can be seen by comparing photographs of the narrow strip fields at Wardlow (Derbyshire), taken in 1982 and 2016. However, the downward spiral of decay has been reversed in recent decades, with the upsurge in interest in walling among both farmers and volunteers in the conservation movement. The work of the Dry Stone Walling Association of Great Britain, founded in Galloway in 1968, is contributing to the preservation of the wallers' skills and a re-emergence of pride in local styles of walling.

2

'Reading' Dry Stone Walls: A Field Guide

Many dry stone walls continue to form part of the living farming landscape, and are regularly repaired and rebuilt to ensure that they remain stock-proof. However, as features of the upland landscape that have their roots deep in the past, walls often preserve in their fabric evidence of past farming practice. By careful observation, it is possible to 'read' dry stone walls as historical documents, noting minor features, which, though often now redundant, preserve a legacy of former times. This chapter aims to provide a field guide to finding the history locked into dry stone walls.

A: Materials and Construction

Dry stone walls play a major part in determining the character of upland landscapes, and one of the key variables in their visual impact is the type of stone from which the walls of an area are built. Stone is heavy and expensive to transport, and so in almost all cases walls are built of local rock. In Yorkshire the neat, rectangular blocks of millstone grit give a very different character to walls in Wharfedale from that of irregular lumps of moss-covered limestone in Craven, for example. In Cumbria the dark, jagged volcanic rocks of the central Lake District produce walls that strongly contrast with the glowing rust-red of Permo-Triassic sandstone in the Eden valley. Where underlying geology changes over a short distance, the fabric of the walls reflects this.

From an historical viewpoint, a key difference cuts across the geology, namely the source of the building materials. In broad terms, a distinction may be drawn between 'field stones' – that is, loose stones that have been picked up from the land – and quarried stone, where stones have been cut from an outcrop of bedrock. Field stones are generally water-worn or smoothed by glacial action; quarried stones are sharp and angular. Since field stones have often been brought some distance by ice or water, they can provide geological variety in a short stretch of wall, particularly where glacial erratics have been deposited from several miles away. Both field stones and quarried stone can be found in the same stretch of wall: indeed, stones in glacial deposits can be angular, and wall builders might break field stones into smaller pieces, producing cut edges. However, there is a broad correlation between field stones and walls in older farmland

Millstone grit enclosure wall at Hebden in Wharfedale, on moorland enclosed in the 1850s. Regular courses of gritstone blocks laid horizontally up the steep slope and topped with shaped capstones.

and between quarried stone and walls built during the era of Parliamentary enclosure. Early modern walls that divided a community's arable fields and meadows served an important secondary function as absorbers of stones cleared from the fields, either during cultivation or in a more deliberate programme of clearance. Valley-bottom walls thus generally contain a high proportion of rounded stones. In contrast, a combination of the need to construct walls dividing Parliamentary enclosure allotments quickly and the fact that much of the land being enclosed was rough hill land that would not be cultivated meant that stone was quarried for these walls. The quality of Parliamentary enclosure walls depended in large part on the quality of the stone available: regular squared blocks of sandstone or millstone grit often produced walls that are still sound, whereas the thin, friable fragments of Skiddaw slate in the northern Lake District, for example, were difficult to work with and could produce unstable walls.

Aesthetics and pride in good workmanship no doubt played a part in the development of distinctive regional walling styles. Even though the nature of the available stone was the major determinant in the character of a wall, similar raw materials could be used in different ways. The main opportunities to enhance the line and evenness of a wall

Carboniferous limestone near Ingleton, North Yorkshire. Irregular blocks of moss-encrusted limestone, roughly coursed.

Boulders and slate at Tarn Hows in the Lake District. Field stones held in a matrix of thin layers of slate.

Permo-Triassic sandstone near Lazonby in the Eden Valley, Cumbria.

Field stone wall at Chapel-le-Dale, near Ingleton, North Yorkshire, composed of a mixture of limestone and gritstone, irregular in size and shape and rounded by the actions of water and ice.

Quarried stone wall on former common land at Kingsdale, North Yorkshire, enclosed in 1819.

lay in choosing uniform capstones and using the 'throughs' to add a projecting band to the face of the wall. The materials that lent themselves most readily to such decorative ends were the sandstones, both the Permo-Triassic red sandstone and the Carboniferous Millstone Grit. The classic gritstone walls of the Yorkshire Pennines, built of squared blocks of stone, sometimes with shaped capstones or with two rows of projecting 'throughs', are perhaps the ultimate in deliberate design.

Not all double walls follow the standard pattern. As noted earlier, the use of orthostats (stones placed 'on their backs', rather than being bedded horizontally) seems to be associated with older forms of wall construction. Where suitably large slabs of stone could be quarried, they might be used in combination with traditional walling techniques, as at Scales, near Ingleton, North Yorkshire, where massive, irregular pieces of limestone have been prised from nearby limestone pavement and placed orthostatically to form the lower sections of a wall. There was a settled community at Scales by 1251, and it is tempting to see these walls, which enclose small, irregularly shaped fields, as dating from initial colonisation in the medieval period. A very different form of orthostatic walling from a more recent period is found in parts of the Scottish Highlands, where some nineteenth-century walls contain facing stones placed vertically. At first sight, their smooth faces appear to be composed of large boulders but, on inspection, these are found to have little depth, instead relying on being skilfully locked with packing stones.

Wall with two rows of projecting 'throughs' near Addingham, West Yorkshire.

Massive limestone orthostats in a wall at Scales, near Ingleton, North Yorkshire, prized from a limestone pavement nearby.

Nineteenth-century wall with facing stones set vertically, Kilbride, Isle of Skye.

Regional varieties

Galloway dykes. One does not have to travel far across upland Britain to appreciate that other forms of dry stone wall construction are possible. In south-west Scotland the standard wall is the 'Galloway dyke' (sometimes called a 'snap-dyke'), which consists of a normal double wall in its lower courses, above which is a single wall (the 'snap' in some eighteenth-century sources), described by F. Rainsford-Hannay as 'big, rough stones, laid and interlocking and narrowing towards the top, but with wide interstices between them and the *light showing through*'. The author of the agricultural report on Midlothian in 1793 described Galloway dykes as 'formidable looking' structures: 5 feet (152 cm) high, built double to around 30 inches (75 cm) high, followed by a cover band ('a thin course of flat stones') projecting 3 inches (8 cm) on either side, above which was a single wall consisting of 'rugged round stones' tapering towards the top. The Galloway dyke builds on the observation that livestock will not attempt to jump or climb a structure through which they can see light: as the early-nineteenth-century county agricultural report for Inverness-shire put it, walls of this nature 'have such a tottering and alarming appearance that all kinds of stock are terrified to attempt them.' The style seems to have originated in Galloway in the early eighteenth century and had spread

Galloway dyke near Craigmuie, Balmaclellan, Galloway. A comparatively low example, merely 3 feet, 6 inches (1.07 m) high, consisting of a low double wall topped by around 24 inches (60 cm) of single wall, through which light can be seen.

widely during the age of improvement. They had reached Renfrewshire and the Isle of Man by the 1760s. In 1767 a waller was employed to surround the estate at Cornaa, near Maughold, on the Isle of Man, with a stone dyke, which was clearly conceived as a Galloway dyke. The section of the wall on the hillside was to be 6 feet (1.8 m) high and 30 inches (76 cm) wide at the base, tapering to 17 inches (43 cm) at the top. The lower 4 feet (122 cm) were to be built as a double dyke and the upper 2 feet (61 cm) as 'snap'. Another section of the wall, running by the river, was to be 4 feet, 6 inches (137 cm) high, with 3 feet (90 cm) of double dyke and 18 inches (45 cm) of 'snap'.[20] By the 1790s Galloway dykes were to be found across the Borders and in the Ochil Hills, and they had spread north to the Highlands by the early nineteenth century.

Galloway dykes were not the only type of single walling. Where large boulders, particularly of granite, were available through field clearance, entire single walls are found, making use of the same principle that sheep will not attempt to jump if light shows. Such 'boulder dykes' are not uncommon in Scotland and Ireland, with perhaps the pinnacle of single walling being in the townlands fringing the Mourne Mountains in Northern Ireland. In northern England little single walling is found and ambivalence towards it is perhaps suggested by the term 'jammy' walls, which is encountered in south-west Cumbria and implies that it is only luck that keeps them standing!

Single boulder wall in townland of Moneydorragh More Upper, near Annalong, Co. Down. (© Eric Jones)

Single walling blocking a gate opening at Chapel-le-Dale, near Ingleton, North Yorkshire.

Consumption walls. During the eighteenth and nineteenth centuries, exceptionally wide walls were built in parts of north-east Scotland as a way of consuming the vast volume of stone cleared from fields as they were reclaimed for cultivation. The most famous are those in Aberdeenshire, particularly the dykes at Kingswells, west of Aberdeen, which were built in the 1850s, the most massive of which is 440 m long, 10 m wide and 2 m high, with a paved path running down its length. Few others are so striking – a wall such as that at Kingswells presupposed clearance for arable cultivation and required a large input of capital and labour. However, more modest consumption walls are found in upland areas as well, where field clearance produced large quantities of stone. For example, the limited, and hence precious, expanses of flat dale-bottom land suitable for cultivation in valleys such as those at Wasdale Head and Eskdale in the Lake District contain bulging sections of wall, built to absorb large quantities of small, water-worn stones cleared from the fields.

Stone slab fences. One of the most striking ways of using stone to create a stock-proof boundary was to place vertical slabs of stone side by side – an inventive way of using local resources, where a suitably fissile rock could be split into large pieces. Slab fences are widely distributed and go by a variety of names: they are found in the Devonian 'Old Red' sandstone flagstones of Caithness and Orkney, in the Skiddaw slates and Silurian mudstones of the Lake District (where they are sometimes referred to as 'shard' fences),

Consumption dyke at Kingswells, Aberdeenshire, probably dating from the 1850s. (© Colin Smith)

Consumption wall at Boot, Eskdale, Cumbria, built to absorb stones cleared from the fields.

in the slates of Snowdonia and the Silurian flags of Radnorshire, and in the Oolitic limestone of the Cotswolds (where they known as 'limestone plank fences'). In north-east Lancashire slab fences of heavy sandstone are known as 'vaccary walls', the suggestion being that they were associated with lordly cattle farms of the medieval period. In fact, there is no evidence whatsoever of a link between slab fences and vaccaries. At Wycoller, the location of what are probably the best-known 'vaccary walls', there were indeed two vaccaries in the middle ages, but the slab fences near Height Laithe, which form the boundaries of long, rectangular fields on the northern side of the Wycoller valley, are unlikely to be of medieval date. The boundaries have the appearance of post-medieval enclosure and subdivision of the valley-side pastures. Indeed, it has been suggested that they date from the eighteenth or early nineteenth century. The name 'vaccary wall' seems to have spread to other parts of the Pennines, where similar slab fences are found, such as near Edenfield and Bradford.

The slab fences of the Lake District are particularly numerous in the Silurian Brathay flags around Hawkshead, where they are particularly common along roadsides and other routeways, often being supplemented by hedges. The slabs are fashioned so they partly overlap each other, creating a continuous solid face, with each stone locked into its neighbours. Again, a comparatively recent date is probable; the 1799 enclosure award for land at Claife, overlooking Windermere, specified that the enclosure wall was to be 4 feet, 6 inches (137 cm) high, 'unless made with flaggs', in which case it might be 3 feet 6 inches (107 cm). Meanwhile, in Hawkshead, map evidence shows that some flag fences date from the middle decades of the nineteenth century. Most of these slab

'Vaccary wall' at Wycoller, Lancashire.

Slab fence (or 'shard fence') at Hawkshead, Cumbria, composed of carefully interlocking slabs of Silurian mudstone.

fences are around 3 feet, 6 inches (107 cm) high, suggesting that, though any connection with vaccaries is almost certainly spurious, their purpose may nevertheless have been to control cattle, rather than sheep.

Stone and earth combinations. Most hedge banks (termed 'cast dykes' – that is, banks created by casting up earth – in northern England) contain a proportion of stone; at the very least, they acted as a dumping ground for stones ploughed up in the course of cultivation. However, some deliberately combined stone and earth to create distinctive regional styles of field boundary. Throughout the west of the British Isles there was a long tradition of constructing such banks. They range from earthen banks containing a greater or lesser proportion of stone to the stone-breasted banks recorded in sixteenth-century northern England (see p. 27–8). The *cloddiau* of Wales (*clawdd* is simply the Welsh for 'dyke') – like the 'Cornish hedges', 'Dartmoor hedges' or 'Devon hedges' of south-west England, and 'hedged ditches' of Ireland – consist of earthen cores faced with stone, allowing vegetation to grow in the core, forming an integral part of the boundary. Comparable boundaries are found in coastal areas of north-west England; along the Cumbrian coast, for example, turf and stone banks are found, using sea-worn cobbles from the shore, interlaid with layers of turf to construct a solid, if low, bank that could be surmounted by a hedge (sometimes of gorse) or a post and wire fence to create a stock-proof barrier.

A Devon hedge at Croyde, North Devon.

Stone-faced earth bank on the Cumbrian coast near St Bees Head.

The regional styles discussed above are by no means comprehensive: stones have been set vertically or in herring-bone patterns to create local styles of walling that are very different from the standard dry stone wall. Indeed, the standard style of wall associated with Parliamentary enclosure (and the Galloway dyke, its equivalent in Scotland in the age of improvement) did not completely dislodge local and regional variation.

B: Functional Features

Walls were and are part of the working farm landscape, functional barriers that divide the land into parcels for separate uses or mark ownership. The walls themselves preserve numerous features, some now redundant, that recall aspects of day-to-day farming practice. Identifying these helps in understanding how the landscape worked.

Many walls were topped by capstones (called 'cams' in Cumbria; 'capes' in the North Riding; 'combers' in the Cotswolds) laid on edge along the top course of the wall. Not only did they give the wall a look of completion, but they also served a very practical purpose. Laid asymmetrically, so that one end projected beyond the face of the wall,

Capstones (called 'cams' in Cumbria) on a wall near Ullswater, projecting on the side of the wall facing the common (to the left) as an additional deterrent to keep sheep from the intake on the right.

they acted as a further deterrent to livestock – an overhanging top course to warn sheep against jumping. The side on which the capstones overhang indicates the direction from which the wall was intended to deter stock. Thus, the capstones of an intake wall adjoining the common would project against the open hillside, so as to deter sheep from entering the enclosed land.

All walls required entrance ways to provide access between fields. Many gateways remain the standard 5- to 6-foot (1.5- to 1.8 m) opening of the nineteenth and twentieth centuries. Increasing numbers have been rebuilt to accommodate the needs of progressively wider vehicles: gateways in active use by the grass-harvesting machinery used in connection with modern large round bales can now be up to 5 m wide. Evidence of rebuilding and widening includes the replacement of one or both gate posts by modern materials, traces of newer walling to infill behind a gatepost, and heaps of superfluous stone left over when the end of the wall has been taken down. Earlier entrances could be narrower and sometimes survive, or can be identified where they have been blocked. Whereas many hay meadows would have required an entrance wide enough for a horse-drawn haywain from the eighteenth century, narrower gateways would have sufficed elsewhere, where no more than access on foot or on horseback was required. Entrances as little as 3 feet (0.9m) wide are sometimes still found. Nor should

Modern gateway at Longsleddale, Cumbria. Walls are increasingly taken back to provide the wide field entrances required by modern machinery.

Narrow gateway (approximately 3 feet wide) at Gunnerside pasture, Swaledale.

we forget the former prevalence of sledges in upland northern England for carting a wide range of burdens including hay, peat for fuel, or bracken for livestock bedding, for example. Entrances wide enough for a 3-foot sled were needed for such purposes.

Just as the width of a gateway can be a reminder of past farming practice, the variety of materials and style of construction of gate stoops can also reflect past usage. Gate stoops represented expensive elements in a field boundary, usually requiring a pair of large and specially cut stones. Slate stoops, either won from local outcrops that were known to yield slabs that would cleave into large pieces or bought in from specialist quarries, are common in the Lake District. It was far more difficult to obtain suitably large, neat stoops from the limestone of Yorkshire or Derbyshire, but some are found. In all areas, professionally made sandstone stoops became common during the nineteenth century; these machine-cut, regular-sized posts frequently continue to serve as gateposts today. In some areas, alternatives to traditional gate stoops are found. In upper Wensleydale and Mallerstang, for example, massive gate piers were built from squared stones that were similar in size to those used on the walls, giving a humble field gate the look of a formal entrance to the grounds of a Victorian villa.

From the late eighteenth century most wall openings carried conventional gates that were hung on metal hinges set in lead, in holes drilled into the stoop. Earlier forms of entrance were designed to avoid the need for expensive metalwork or a costly piece of stone as a gate stoop. Harr-hung gates enabled a gate to be hung without the need for

Slate outcrop in fields at Loweswater. Oral tradition held that this outcrop was quarried for large slabs of slate for use as gate stoops and stall divisions in byres. It probably also supplied stone for the sections of slab fence found in roadside walls nearby.

Rough dolomitic limestone gatepost at Roystone Grange, Derbyshire, probably of an early date.

Shaped sandstone gatepost at Ullswater in the Lake District, probably brought in from a stonemason's yard in the Penrith area in the nineteenth century.

Pair of gateposts of a type found widely in the millstone grit of Wensleydale, built as freestanding structures. These examples are at Widdale, near Hawes.

a large and expensive stoop. The gate pivoted on iron pintles that were set vertically into drilled stones, projecting from the wall at the top and bottom. The protruding stone carrying the upper pintle was sometimes kept in place by a massive boulder on the wall top, with the lower fixture being set into a pad stone, which is often now obscured by vegetation. An earlier form of harr-hung gate is probably to be associated with a distinctive form of gate stoop found in the south Pennines, which is perforated near the top by a single square hole, perhaps 3 inches (75 mm) across. John Farey, author of the county agricultural report for Derbyshire in 1813, appears to record such gates. 'Anciently, the Gates in the Peak Hundreds were formed and hung without any iron-work', he wrote, noting that some remained in Birchover and other places. 'A large mortise-hole is made thro' the hanging-post ... at about four feet and a half high, into which a stout piece of wood is firmly wedged, and projects about twelve inches before the Post'. The wood was drilled to take the two ends of 'a tough piece of green Ash or Sallow', forming a bow that held the projecting upper arm of the gate.[21]

Another type of moveable barrier, formerly common, was the use of wooden bars or rails, which could be removed when access was needed. This obviated the need for metal fixtures but required specially made gate stoops. The rails were slotted into stoops on either side, and it is these distinctive stone gate stoops, fashioned to take rails, that

Harr-hung gate near Wasdale Head, Cumbria. The projecting stone is drilled to take the upper pintle; the lower pintle is held in a stone in the ground (hidden by vegetation).

Gate stoop near Addingham, drilled with a single squared hole, of a type found in the south Pennines. The hole may have carried a wooden peg to support a harr-hung gate.

survive, often reused to carry a gate. Two distinct designs are found in northern England, reflecting differences in the ease of working the stone from which they were hewn. In the slates of the Lake District, they take the form of four or five holes into which the wooden bars could be slotted. The thickness of the slate, or a space between the stoop and the wall end, allowed the bars to be slid sideways to release one end for removal. In the gritstone country of the south Pennines, by contrast, where stone could be cut and carved more readily, one stoop carried grooved slots into which the bars could be fitted horizontally, while the other had a series of round depressions sufficient to hold the other end of the bars. Both variants served the same purpose and are a reminder that opening and closing fields traditionally occurred on a seasonal basis. A hay meadow would be closed to livestock in the spring and only reopened when the hay was cut; access was not needed on a daily basis, meaning bars could be put in place in April and only removed in July. More generally, they are a legacy of the division of the early-modern farming year into a 'closed' season during the spring and summer, when crops were growing, and an 'open' season in the winter months, when stock was allowed to graze freely across the fields. Field entrances taking the form of a set of bars were adequate for this seasonal pattern of opening and closure.

Other reminders of movement between fields include stiles (for humans) and smouts (for animals). Rights of way across the fields, from outlying farms to church, for example, were often established at an early date and had to be respected by enclosure

Slate gate stoops drilled to take wooden bars at Troutbeck, Cumbria. A rare survival of a traditional means of closing a gateway.

Gritstone gate stoop near High Brockabank, Addingham, West Yorkshire, with slots to take bars. Note how the two curved slots are on opposite sides, perhaps to make it more difficult for livestock to dislodge all the bars.

walls. Stiles were, therefore, often built into walls at the time of construction. Two of the most common forms were through stones of sufficient length to project on either side, creating steps to allow the wall to be climbed, and the 'squeeze stile', a narrow gap between two vertical slabs. Stiles thus enabled movement between fields without disrupting the stock-proof capacity of the walls.

Allowing selected livestock to pass through a wall, often on a seasonal basis, was the function of small rectangular openings in the lower courses of a wall. These go by various names: the generic term is 'smout' or 'smoot', but there are regional variants such as 'lunky hole' in southern Scotland and 'cripple hole' in Yorkshire. They served a variety of purposes; the majority were for sheep, but there were also 'water smoots', where a wall crossed a minor water course, and 'rabbit smoots' to lure rabbits into a trap set into the ground on one side of the opening. 'Sheep creeps' allowed sheep to pass through the wall from one field to the next and could be closed by blocking the opening with a boulder, flagstone or slate. They enabled seasonal control of grazing, as shown by an order from the manor court at Ousby on the edge of the north Pennines in 1683, which required the 'smoughts' to be opened yearly on 20 November and to be closed again on 1 March.[22] In the Lake District, the term 'hogg hole' is a reminder of what was probably the chief purpose of smouts

Stile created from projecting slate 'throughs' near Ambleside, Cumbria.

Squeeze stile where a footpath crosses a wall in old farmland at Hebden in Wharfedale.

Water smout near Horton-in-Ribblesdale, North Yorkshire, allowing a small stream to flow under a wall. Unusually, this is a 'two-storey' smout, so as to cope with the rapid changes in water flow that occur in limestone country.

Sheep creep (or 'cripple hole') near Hebden in Wharfedale, blocked with a large flagstone that would be removed on a seasonal basis to allow sheep to pass through.

in that environment, to allow young sheep ('hoggs') to graze across several fields during their first winter.

Another functional feature, making use of the shelter provided by a dry stone wall, was the bee bole, a rectangular recess in the face of a south- or south-east-facing wall that provided a shelf for a traditional bee 'skep'. Bee boles are often found in groups and, as might be expected, in walls surrounding gardens and orchards. Some are considerably larger than the traditional skep (which was typically 10–15 inches (25–38 cm) in diameter and 7–15 inches (18–38 cm) high), providing space for bracken to be packed around the skep to protect the colony over winter. As with all aspects of dry stone walls, dating bee boles is difficult: most are thought to have been built in the seventeenth to nineteenth centuries.

Dry stone walling was also used to build what may be thought of as the 'furniture' of livestock farming in the uplands, the variety of sheepfolds and other structures found in stone-walled landscapes. Folds came in a variety of forms, with different purposes. First were the formal pinfolds, part of the structure of manorial administration, in which livestock that had strayed onto grazing grounds to which they had no right were impounded until a fee (termed 'pound loose' in parts of northern England) was paid by the owner of the offending beasts. Building pinfolds was a communal responsibility,

'Hogg-hole' in a wall at Rydal in the Lake District to allow young sheep ('hoggs') to move between fields.

Bee boles at Troutbeck, Cumbria. 'Skeps' (beehives) were set on shelves as in the middle recess here. (© Chris Bratt, Dry Stone Walling Association (Cumbria Branch))

Pinfold at Loweswater, Cumbria. The small square enclosure was on the boundary between the farmland (to the right of this photograph) and the open fell (to the left; now wooded).

required by the lord of the manor. The manor court would appoint a 'pinder' or 'pounder', whose job it was to bring stray animals to the fold and to care for them until the fee was paid. Pinfolds are recorded from the medieval period, though most are probably of eighteenth- or nineteenth-century date in their present form. They are usually small enclosures – some are circular, others rectangular, and around 10 m to 20 m in diameter – and tend to be found on the edge of a village or on the margin of common land, and close to a supply of water to serve the impounded livestock.

Other sheepfolds were private folds, used to manage sheep at key points in the shepherding year. Essentially, they were for holding sheep to enable them to be sorted. Some large folds on upland commons were used for sorting the livestock of different owners when the common was driven periodically, not least to identify 'foreign' sheep that had strayed from other commons. On some upland pastures a system of 'agistment' was found, where payments for grazing were made and livestock needed to be sorted to confirm ownership. A large fold, known as the Mountain Pinfold, on Stockdale Moor, between Wasdale and Ennerdale in the Lake District, is a legacy of such a system. In the seventeenth and eighteenth centuries the moor was driven annually on 8 September ('Lady Day in Harvest') to determine agistment fees and the livestock was held in the fold until payment had been made.

Sheepfold on Scales Moor, North Yorkshire.

Washfold beside Hollow Moss Beck, Dunnerdale, Cumbria. The smaller pen opened onto a pool formed by damming the beck in the foreground. The wall extending behind would have assisted in gathering the flock into the fold.

Other folds on common land were washfolds, where sheep were penned at washing time and the fleeces were washed in fresh water to clean them before shearing. Placed beside a watercourse – either a naturally deep pool or somewhere a 'wash dub' could be created by damming the stream, washfolds can be identified by having an exit opening onto the pool – for sheep, there was only one way out of the fold!

As well as folds for livestock management, there were a range of stone-walled structures built for shelter. One distinctive variant of the sheepfold was the stell, a small circular pen, which was usually around 10 m wide, with a single small opening on one side. Stells were a quintessential part of the sheep-rearing husbandry of both the Scottish Borders, where they are recorded from the mid-eighteenth century, and the Northumberland Cheviots. In at least one instance a Border shepherd took the idea with him to Somerset: a circular stell at Three Combes Foot, near Larkbarrow on Exmoor, was built by a Dumfriesshire shepherd in 1878.[23]

The hill grazings also contained a variety of smaller dry-stone structures offering shelter to livestock, to which the generic term 'bield' was given. Many are short sections of dry stone walling, perhaps 5 to 8 m in length, placed to provide shelter from the prevailing wind. Their use by sheep over many a cold winter is often attested by a rich growth of nettles, thriving on the accumulated urine and droppings on the leeward side. More sophisticated forms are found: some bields take the form of longer, curved

Stell on the slopes of Meikle Shag in the Lowther Hills of Lanarkshire.

Bield near Askrigg in Wensleydale. This example shows two building phases: the main section with projecting throughs seems to have been extended to the left by a wall without projecting stones.

pieces of wall; L-shaped bields are widespread; and cross-walls, providing shelter from all directions, are not uncommon, particularly in the Scottish Borders. Most are almost impossible to date but the tradition of building bields in the Pennines goes back to the sixteenth century at least, as references to 'buildwalls' in Teesdale in a lawsuit of 1575 make clear.[24]

C: Ownership

Responsibility for the upkeep of field boundaries that were also boundaries between properties has long been spelt out in title deeds. If a boundary between two properties was shared between the owners, they might each be allocated responsibility for half of the length. Each might decide to make their section of the boundary in a different way: all that mattered was that it should be stock-proof. If one owner preferred a well-laid hedge while his neighbour opted for a dry stone wall, the result could be a mixture of different boundary types. The short sections of dry stone wall that are sometimes found between lengths of hedge or fence may be legacies of past patterns of responsibility.

Wall-head in the wall surrounding Gunnerside pasture, Swaledale, North Yorkshire. The initials 'DC', carved into a stone near the base, indicate who was responsible for the section of wall beginning at this wall-head.

Where the whole length of a boundary took the form of a dry stone wall, the pattern of responsibility for maintenance was sometimes physically embedded within it. The point where ownership changed was often marked by a vertical straight joint or 'wall head.' These are particularly common in walls built as a result of Parliamentary enclosure, where the enclosure award spelt out responsibility for maintenance of field boundaries in great detail. They are also found in earlier generations of walls, notably those surrounding communally owned pasture closes, such as the cow pastures and other stinted pastures found widely in the Yorkshire Pennines. One of the most remarkable is the wall along Tinkers' Lane that marks the boundary between Grassington and Hebden townships in Wharfedale. It seems to have divided the stinted pastures belonging to the two villages: Hebden's pasture had been recently enclosed in 1600, which suggests a possible date for its construction. The wall is divided into short sections, one chain (22 yards; 20.5 m) in length, marked by wall heads where responsibility for its upkeep changed. Many of the wall heads carry initials (or occasionally a symbol) carved into a prominent stone. From the few instances where the form of a carved letter provides evidence of dating, a broadly seventeenth-century date seems likely.

Wall-head at Tinkers' Lane, Hebden in Wharfedale. One of a series of straight edges at 22-yard intervals, marking changes in responsibility for the upkeep of the wall. The initials 'WR' carved into a stone on the left of the wall-head probably date from the seventeenth century.

Dated gate stoop at Ulpha in the Duddon valley, Cumbria. The initials 'IG' are probably those of a member of the Gunson family of Church House.

By their nature as humble, functional features composed of small pieces of stone, dry stone walls do not lend themselves to the same sort of proud statements of ownership that are found on houses and barns. Almost the only features along the length of a wall that could carry an inscription of any length were the gate stoops, which generally took the form of slabs of sandstone or slate. Most of these are unadorned, but occasionally the face of a stoop has been used to carry initials and a date. Two examples from the Lake District are on stoops made to take bars, rather than a conventional gate, and both date from the heyday of wall building in the century from 1750 to 1850. One, at the entrance to a field beside Ulpha church in the Duddon valley, carries the date 1766 and the initials 'I G', probably those of John or Joseph Gunson of Church House. The carving is firm but rather rustic, suggesting that Gunson may have cut the inscription himself, perhaps to mark the completion of a piece of wall-building or renewal around his fields. The second example comes from Buttermere and bears the inscription 'I. C. 1829'. Again identification is possible, the initials probably being those of John Clark of Syke House, Buttermere. The last number of the date seems to have been changed from '0' to '9'. John Clark of Buttermere died in 1829 – perhaps the inscription was modified to record the year of his death, in effect converting a gatepost into a memorial.

Dated gate stoop at Buttermere, Cumbria. The initials 'IC' are probably those of John Clark of Syke House.

D: Legacies of the Past

Both the fabric of a dry stone wall and the course it follows are worthy of careful observation, since both may preserve evidence of other aspects of the past.

Reuse of building materials. Notwithstanding the over-abundance of stones from field clearance in some areas, finding sufficient stone could often present a challenge, and wallers might quarry masonry from demolished buildings and other structures. Particularly striking examples of this are to be found in the vicinity of Roman sites. Many field walls along the line of Hadrian's Wall contain the distinctive squared sandstone blocks shaped by Roman masons, as do walls adjacent to Roman forts across northern England. Other archaeological sites have been robbed for field walls: a Neolithic stone circle known as Grey Yauds, which stood on heather moorland near Cumwhitton in north-east Cumbria, was broken up and its stones used to build the new enclosure walls when the moorland was divided in 1801. The larger fragments, used for the foundations, give these comparatively recent walls a misleading look of antiquity. Several miles to the south, at Shap, large granite boulders that formed part of

Roman masonry reused in a field wall, near Banks on Hadrian's Wall. A large squared facing stone from the Roman Wall is visible in the centre of the photograph.

a megalithic stone avenue have been incorporated into the walls enclosing the former open fields, the great size of some of them ensuring that they remain intact.

More modest stones from a domestic, vernacular context are frequently found built into walls, such as shaped and dressed fragments of door and window surrounds, roofing flags and slates. Large worked stones could be particularly valuable for use as throughs. Examples of such reuse include the broken millstones incorporated into walls near quarrying sites on the millstone grit of the Pennines and broken granite hand querns of medieval or earlier date, which have been found in field walls in both the Yorkshire Dales and the Lake District. Clay tobacco pipes and other objects are from time to time discovered in the filling of walls, sometimes intact, perhaps indicating that they were placed their deliberately by the waller as a sort of signature or 'time capsule'. Since the shape of pipe bowls allows them to be dated quite closely, such finds can enable a building phase of a wall to be dated.

Sometimes reuse of materials from a demolished building can also help to date a wall. One example will suffice: a minor road near Loweswater in the northern Lake District runs past the site of the small corn mill that served the township of Brackenthwaite, demolished in the later nineteenth century. The wall flanking the lane where it passes the site of the mill is unexceptional but its comparatively recent date is shown by the fact that broken pieces of perforated tile from the corn-drying kiln attached to the mill are incorporated into the wall. Checking the early editions of the Ordnance Survey Six Inch

Broken hand quern of medieval or earlier date in a field wall in the Newlands valley, near Keswick, Cumbria.

Deliberate deposits? Two finds from the depths of dry stone walls in north-west Yorkshire: a late-nineteenth-century inkpot carefully placed and protected by a stone; and the bowl of a 'Tom White' pipe, made for Irish workmen, dating from *c*. 1870. The pipe was found in a wall beside the Settle & Carlisle Railway and was probably deposited by an Irish navvie. (Courtesy of David Johnson, Settle)

map confirms that the road lay open to the mill and its yard in the 1860s but that the line of the wall was in place by 1898.

Lines dictated by the past. The course taken by a wall was often dictated by pre-existing lines in the landscape, as, for example, where the edges of furlongs and strips in an open field are perpetuated in the lines of walls that divided it on enclosure (see pp. 30–1). It is thus possible to, as it were, read through the pattern of field walls to recapture older patterns of land use and ownership. Two further examples (walls that follow older boundary lines, and walls that incorporate lost buildings) illustrate this point.

Long sections of civil parish boundaries in the northern uplands are followed by dry stone walls built during the great wave of Parliamentary enclosure of moorland and hill in the nineteenth century. In these cases the line of the parish boundary (generally replicating a much older township and manorial boundary) determined the line taken

Earthenware tile from a corn-drying kiln at Brackenthwaite Mill, near Loweswater, Cumbria, which was built into a wall that was constructed in the later nineteenth century when the mill was demolished.

by the enclosure wall, since it marked the limits of the manor, whose wastes were being enclosed. In consequence, a wall along a parish boundary may incorporate older boundary markers, dating from the pre-enclosure period when the boundary between two communities ran over open moorland.

Sometimes the antiquity of a boundary marker could be considerable, predating the building of an enclosure wall by many centuries. 'Navelin Stone', a large glacial erratic boulder on Longbarrow Moss to the north-east of Egremont, Cumbria, was one of the fixed points on the boundary between Brisco and Cleator, spelt out in a charter of *c*. 1210 (when its name – possibly already ancient – was recorded as 'Auenelestan'). It remained a boundary marker on a fairly featureless open hillside until the enclosure of the commons of Brisco and Cleator in 1783 and 1825 respectively, when it became fossilised in a new enclosure wall (which has since collapsed) following the ancient boundary.

Some moorland boundaries remained undefined – or even disputed between adjacent communities – until shortly before enclosure. For example, the long-uncertain boundary across wide, bleak moorland between Stainmore in Westmorland and Lune Forest in

'Navelin Stone' near Egremont, Cumbria, in 1976, before afforestation. The boulder was named as a boundary marker in a charter of *c*. 1210. When Brisco and Cleator commons were enclosed (in 1783 and 1825 respectively), a new wall (tumbled and decayed by the time this photograph was taken) was built along the boundary, incorporating the ancient boundary stone.

the North Riding remained in contention in the late eighteenth century, with matters coming to a head in a dispute over mineral royalties in relation to a mine at Silver Keld Well in the 1790s. The boundary was finally defined in the early nineteenth century (probably in the 1830s) and marked by a line of numbered boundary stones across the empty wastes around Mickle Fell. When Stainmore Common was regulated and enclosed in 1879, the new wall along the parish boundary followed the boundary stones, which survived alongside it.

Buildings are an integral part of the pattern of fields and lanes, and the walls of farm buildings and other outbuildings often double up as field boundaries. Farmsteads can be thought of as hubs in the field pattern, linked by lanes and tracks to outlying fields and other settlements. The network of field boundaries generally becomes denser around farmsteads, where yards, gardens, orchards and paddocks ('garths,' 'crofts' and 'parrocks' in the traditional language of the northern English countryside) create a pattern of small enclosures. Buildings – both dwellings and agricultural buildings – come and go and, in areas of dry stone walls, they often leave a visible trace. When a building fell out of use and into decay, it obviously made sense to continue to use its walls in a field boundary, meaning that fabric from long-lost dwellings can be found

Boundary wall of North Stainmore Common at Silver Keld Well, probably built around 1879. It followed the county boundary between Westmorland and the North Riding of Yorkshire, which remained disputed until the early nineteenth century, when it was marked by a line of boundary stones across the unenclosed moorland (seen here beside the wall).

incorporated into a stretch of dry stone wall. Two examples illustrate the potential of marrying detailed field observation with archival research to explain what at first sight appear to be unusual features in the line taken by a wall.

The first comes from the head of Miterdale, a small, narrow valley tucked into the Lake District fells between Eskdale and Wasdale. Settlement has drained away from the upper reaches of Miterdale since the seventeenth century. In 1578 there were six holdings there; by the mid-nineteenth century the number had reduced to three and by the twentieth, only one remained inhabited. One of the deserted holdings, known as Sword House, was purchased by the tenant of a neighbouring farm in 1733 and appears to have ceased to be inhabited by the 1750s. It can still be identified in the footings of two buildings, either side of a small garth, with the gable end and one side wall of each incorporated into surviving field walls. The right-angled turns in the field pattern are the tell-tale signs of the presence of former buildings and the degraded gables, still standing higher than the field wall on either side, clinch the identification.

Unexpected twists and turns in a field wall are always worth investigating. Walls don't just grow; the line taken by a wall has been the deliberate decision of a waller at some stage in the past. An example of this is seen in the wall bounding Brows Pasture, a small common at Chapel-le-Dale, on the edge of the Yorkshire Dales. The wall separating the common from adjacent meadows broadly follows a sweeping curve but, at a point close to a modern field barn, it veers away from the expected line to create a marked

Site of farmstead of Sword House, Miterdale, Cumbria, deserted in the mid-eighteenth century. The gable ends of two buildings survive in the field walls, one marked by the ranging rod, the other to the right of the picture (which was taken in 1978).

"SWORD HOUSE", MITERDALE HEAD
NY 159 024
June 1978

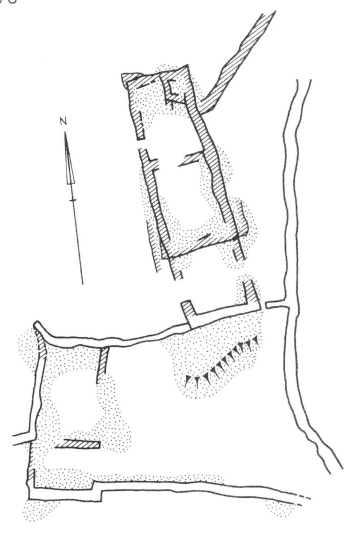

N

Standing drystone wall
Wall footings
Tumbled stones

0   Metres   15

AJLW / VW

Plan of Sword House, Miterdale, surveyed in 1978. (*Transactions of CWAAS,* new series 79 (1979), p. 152)

Deviations in a wall line at Brows Pasture, near Ingleton, North Yorkshire, preserving the memory of lost buildings. Remains of the gable end of one building are visible in the wall to the right of the modern barn; the tithe plan of 1839 shows a second building in the rectangular projection to the right.

protuberance. On inspection, part of this is explained by the position of a former field barn, the gable and side wall of which are incorporated into the field wall, much as at Sword House, Miterdale. Fragments of roofing materials (sandstone flags and slate) built into the wall are further legacies of the barn. Nevertheless, the line taken by the wall suggests that something else has also caused it to stray from its expected course. There is little evidence on the ground (except for what may be an apron of stone spread from a tumbled gable), but the tithe plan of 1839 shows a small garth and a second building, distinct from the former barn.

In both examples, it might be thought that it would have been simpler to straighten out the field boundary once the buildings and garths had ceased to have any function. An important factor here, almost certainly repeated elsewhere where a wall takes an unexpected turn, is that walls often mark the property boundaries. In the case of Brows Pasture, this was the boundary between the individually owned meadows and the common pasture. Landownership can form an inflexible framework, as the boundaries between properties are sacrosanct, causing walls to be maintained or rebuilt along existing lines.

That brings us back to a truism that underlies the topics discussed in this book: every dry stone wall is the product of a deliberate decision to build it in a particular place. Walls are the conscious creations of past generations, prompted by practical farming considerations but also influenced by custom and fashion and the quirks of individual whim. The landscape of dry stone walls today can be thought of as the cumulative product of numberless decisions and many hours of manual labour across the centuries. To the questions posed at the beginning of this book, there is no single answer: the modern landscape of dry stone walls does not date from a single period but is a composite production, reflecting a range of historical processes from the medieval period to the nineteenth century. As this book has sought to show, dry stone walls constitute a landscape legacy rich in historical resonances and are increasingly (and deservedly) coming to be recognised as an important part of the cultural heritage of upland areas. The welcome resurgence of interest in the skill of dry stone walling bodes well for the future.

Notes

1. J. B. Priestley, *English Journey* (Ilkley: Great Northern Books, 2012 [first published 1934]), pp. 135–6.
2. West Yorkshire Archive Service, WYL 524/142; *Coucher Book of Furness Abbey, Vol. II, part ii*, ed. J. Brownbill (Chetham Society new series 76, 1916), p. 296.
3. A. J. L. Winchester, 'Demesne livestock farming in the Lake District: the vaccary at Gatesgarth, Buttermere, in the later thirteenth century', *Transactions of CWAAS*, 3rd series, 3 (2003), pp. 109–18.
4. Brotherton Library (Leeds), Marrick Papers, 3/1/77 (courtesy of Anita Carrieri).
5. Auckland: *Bishop Hatfield's Survey*, ed. W. Greenwell (Surtees Society 32, 1856), p. 214; Thringarth: Essex Record Office, D/DL/M108; Troutbeck: TNA, E178/4690; R. W. Hoyle, 'Thomas first Lord Wharton's parks at Ravenstonedale and Wharton', *Transactions of CWAAS,* new series 95 (1995), pp. 111–18.
6. Yanwath: CAS, WD RY, box 42; Calton: Lancs. Archives, DD Ma, box 9; Shap: J. Whiteside, 'Paines made at Shap', *Transactions of CWAAS*, new series 3 (1903), p. 151.
7. Lune forest: Durham Record Office, D/St/E3/1/6; Renwick: Queen's College (Oxford), Renwick court rolls; Ousby: CAS, WD CRK/M.13.
8. TNA, E134/23 Eliz./East. 15.
9. TNA, E134/18 Eliz./Trin. 3.
10. TNA, E134/16 Chas. I/East. 4.
11. *Lowther Family Estate Books 1617–1675*, ed. C. B. Phillips (Surtees Society 191, 1975), pp. 70, 234, 240, 246, 253.
12. *The Account Book of Clement Taylor of Finsthwaite 1712–1753*, ed. J. D. Martin (Record Society of Lancashire & Cheshire 135, 1997), pp. 9–10, 33, 73–4, 158.
13. *The Diary of Isaac Fletcher of Underwood, Cumberland, 1756–1781*, ed. A. J. L. Winchester (CWAAS Extra Series 27, 1994), pp. 315–17, 332, 350.
14. *Estate and Household Accounts of Sir Daniel Fleming of Rydal, Westmorland, 1688–1701*, ed. B. Tyson (CWAAS Record Series XIII, 2001), pp. 108, 127, 207, 238.
15. CAS, D BEN/3/752.
16. Information courtesy of Dr D. Denman, Lorton.
17. J. Billingsley, *General View of Agriculture of Somerset* (1798), p. 79.
18. North Yorkshire County Record Office, ZOA (MIC 3516/993).

19. *The Diary of Charles Fothergill 1805,* ed. P. Romney (YAS Record Series CXLII, 1984), pp. 113–15.
20. CAS, D CU/5/2.
21. J. Farey, *General View of Agriculture and Minerals of Derbyshire* (1813), p. 92.
22. CAS, WD CRK/M.13, no. 88.
23. E. Jamieson, 'Archaeological survey work at Larkbarrow Farm', *Somerset Archaeology & Natural History,* 2002, pp. 17–26.
24. Durham Record Office, D/St/E3/1/40.

Bibliography

Beaumont, Heather, *Pointers to the Past: the Historical Landscape of Hebden Township, Upper Wharfedale* (YAS Occasional Paper No. 5, 2006).

Charterhouse Environs Research Team, *Can We Date Mendip's Stone Walls?* (unpublished report, 2008).

Countryside Commission, *The Condition of England's Dry Stone Walls* (Countryside Commission Publication No. 482, 1996).

Dennison, E., 'An historic landscape survey: the Swinithwaite estate, West Witton', in R. F. White and P. R. Wilson (eds.), *Archaeology and Historic Landscapes of the Yorkshire Dales* (YAS Occasional Paper No. 2, 2004), pp. 25–37.

Garner, Lawrence, *Dry Stone Walls* (Shire, 1984; 2nd edn 2005).

Heginbottom, J. A., 'Fences and fields: the evolution of the Calderdale rural landscape from prehistoric times to the present day', *Transaction of Halifax Antiquarian Society*, new series 1 (1993), pp. 15–35.

Herring, Peter, 'Medieval fields at Brown Willy, Bodmin Moor', in S. Turner (ed.), *Medieval Devon and Cornwall: Shaping an Ancient Countryside* (Macclesfield, 2006), pp. 78–103.

Hodges, Richard, *Wall-to-Wall History: the Story of Roystone Grange* (London, 1991).

Johnson, David, 'Chapel-le-Dale, North Yorkshire: the making of an upland landscape', *Landscape History*, 36 (1) (2015), pp. 25–45.

Lord, T. C., '"One on two and two on one": preliminary results from a survey of dry stone walls on the National Trust estate at Malham', in R. F. White and P. R. Wilson (eds.), *Archaeology and Historic Landscapes of the Yorkshire Dales* (YAS Occasional Paper No. 2, 2004), pp. 173–86.

Moorhouse, Stephen, 'Anatomy of the Yorkshire Dales: decoding the medieval landscape', in T. G. Manby, S. Moorhouse and P. Ottaway (eds.), *The Archaeology of Yorkshire* (YAS Occasional Paper No. 3, 2003), at pp. 348–52.

Rainsford-Hannay, F., *Dry Stone Walling* (London, 1957; 2nd edn, Stewartry of Kirkcudbright Drystane Dyking Committee, 1972).

Raistrick, Arthur, *Pennine Walls* (Dalesman, first published 1946).

Ramm, H. G., 'Wycoller walls', *Yorkshire Philosophical Society Annual Report 1988*, pp. 77–89.

Rollinson, William, *Lakeland Walls* (Dalesman, 1969).

Spratt, D. A., 'Orthostatic field walls on the North York Moors', *Yorkshire Archaeological Journal*, 60 (1988), pp. 149–57.

Whyte, Ian, *Transforming Fell and Valley: landscape and Parliamentary enclosure in north-west England* (Lancaster, 2003).

Wildgoose, Martin, 'The drystone walls of Roystone Grange', *Archaeological Journal*, 148 (1991), pp. 205–40.

Williams, Michael, 'The enclosure and reclamation of the Mendip Hills, 1770–1870', *Agricultural History Review*, 19 (1971), pp. 65–81.

Winchester, Angus J. L., *The Harvest of the Hills: Rural Life in Northern England and the Scottish Borders, 1400–1700* (Edinburgh, 2000), especially Chapter 3.